In the Old Corps, by the Book

Citadel Cadet Life in the '60s

Edward H. West

Library of Congress Control Number (LCCN): 9781966647645

ISBNs:
eBook: 978-1-966647-62-1
Paperback: 978-1-966647-63-8
Hardback: 978-1-966647-64-5

Published by:
Authors Publishing House
178 Broadway, 3rd Floor, #1343
New York, NY 10001, USA

Main Line: (855) 624-0155
Email: support@authorspublishinghouse.com

Front and back cover illustrations by Edward H. West.
Graphic Arts augmentation by Kevin L. Metzger.

Table of Contents

Cover illustration for *(The) Shako*
Spring, 1964

Preface

The early 1960s were the end of a golden time to come of age in America: Elvis was a civilian again, Richard Nixon was tanning and resting, and Vietnam was a place where Americans were only offering advice. In those years, I was a cadet becoming a man at The Citadel, so it was also the time when my life was clamped in a straitjacket called *The Blue Book*. This literary marvel comprised 86 pages in small type and was the self-described "regulations for the interior discipline of the Corps of Cadets."

Many years later, I found a vintage copy of *The Blue Book of 1960* for sale in someone's garage. In retirement, I returned to *The Blue Book* as a former cadet and a student of history. This book is the result.

I was an editor in my cadet days, so I was not surprised to find errors in *The Blue Book of 1960*. For instance, on page 79 of the index, the issue of "illness on leave or furlough" is addressed in paragraph 47.02. - e. But the last paragraph of regulations in *The Blue Book* is numbered "45." There is no paragraph 47, not to mention 47.02. - e.

More disturbing is a reference to "College Regulations" in paragraph 9.01.:

9. – BARRACKS ADMINISTRATION

9.01. AGENTS: No cadet shall engage in buying or selling or act as an agent for furnishing any article or entertainment without the approval of The Commandant of Cadets (see paragraph 46 College Regulations).

During my four years as a cadet, I was entirely unaware that there was such a thing as "College Regulations" governing my life along with *The Blue Book*.

At The Citadel today, *The Blue Book* is no longer blue - it has a white cover. Also, there is *The White Book* (with a white cover) which clarifies the intentions of *The Blue Book* in more than 100 pages. In the event of conflict, both of these books are over-ruled by *The College Regulations*. I presume these regulations remain unknown to the cadets they regulate.

In the Old Corps in the '60s, our policy was to accept such conundrums as reality and then simply cope. We all knew an actual regulation stated that ignorance of a regulation was no excuse and assumed this was true, whether or not a regulation was unknowable or even actually existed.

In this reminiscence, the photographs are from my personal archive. The vintage artwork is mine, except for one cartoon by Bill Mauldin. I have added a few fresh cartoons and my friend, Kevin Metzger, greatly assisted me with some graphic art revisions.

For those former residents of the Big House who might want to pursue justice, the statute of limitations for complaints is expired:

40. – RIGHTS OF REDRESS

40.02. APPEAL TO THE BOARD OF VISITORS: Should the complaining party be refused redress, he may appeal through the proper channels to the Chairman of the Board of Visitors. Such complaints will be considered only when made within ten days after the complaining party has been refused redress.

21.06. QUIBBLING:

Quibbling is prohibited. Attempting to avoid punishment by evading the issue is a punishable offense.

So if you ever find an old *Blue Book* and discover spelling errors, missing regulations or other injustices, "Fuggedaboutit" (as we would say in the the Old Corps) and suck it up. Besides, "quibbling is prohibited."

West, E.H.
(Former) cadet

Cover illustration for
(The) Shako
Spring, 1965

Fuggedaboutit!

Introduction: My Veteran Teachers

As a kid, I learned that my father couldn't remember when I was born because of a change in the date where he was at the time. News of my birth reached him as his Pacific War submarine was crossing the International Date Line in enemy waters. Other things were on his mind that day.

Many years later, I learned that my father was a member of the "Greatest Generation." The Greatest Generation endured the Depression, then won World War II. Those were hard times for most; often, they were bitter times. Their life experiences had produced the victories at Normandy, Midway and Iwo Jima. This historical perspective is important to my story because it was military veterans who would be my teachers in the '60s and who would influence the upperclassmen who were my role models.

I grew up on or near naval bases where navy brats were prominently enlisted among my friends. Most of us were being raised by fathers with war stories in a culture of military authority. I might vaguely remember some teachers who were kind to me when I was young. But in those years of cold war and universal military draft, it was primarily male veterans, seasoned by social alarms and war, who comprised my faculty after elementary school. The training experienced in boot camps across America apparently ingrained in most of them the authoritarian approach that stiffened my education years later.

The Greatest Generation was one of austerity. As teachers, the men I knew were focused on the mission and results. They offered education without garnishes, presumed discipline, and tested decisively. Those of us who continued in education and had the temerity to engage Those Who Required Listening after high school also acquired stout hearts and straight spines (or else, bad habits and therapists.) I don't ever recall experiencing anything that might resemble a personal, cordial relationship with a teacher beyond high school. Yet I usually had successful, working relationships with them each year as I matured.

In the years following high school, I received the most concentrated dose of authoritarian education as a cadet at The Citadel, the Military College of South Carolina. At The Citadel, the entire faculty was in uniform and served as officers in the South Carolina Unorganized Militia. They wore the gold or silver of their rank on their shoulders, which commanded respect. (The shiny initials of their militia unit on their lapels, however, did not particularly enhance their dignity.)

My experience at The Citadel affected me all of my life. The veteran teachers concentrated in this one place trained me to imitate their attitudes, methods and mannerisms. Their oversight of my education continued in medical school and explains why my years of classes at Charleston in the '60s were much more connected to the culture of Parris Island than to Woodstock. Maintaining the protocols which preserved the superior status of the teacher were as fundamental in my classrooms in the '60s as were the chemical elements of the periodic table in my chemistry courses.

A representative of such an authoritarian educator was a professor of pathology whom I encountered regularly in a cavernous laboratory as a medical student. He was an officer on a warship during the war. Twenty years later, he was the master and commander of his lab and I was one of eighty or so recruits who hoped to become physicians. The pathology course he taught was one of the stormier seas I had to sail. The doctors ahead of me who learned under his scrutiny referred to him as "The Turnip."

The routine of The Turnip's class included an hour of lecture, followed by two hours of sitting on high, backless stools at long slate counters, confronting the mysteries of urine, feces and spinal fluid. During these hours of socializing with the underworld, I met fellow-travelers such as *Plasmodium vivax* (a malaria parasite) and learned how wading in Lake Victoria can give you bladder cancer. I also developed a skill in spotting many black-hearted little critters with a microscope. An assortment of them would be my midnight opponents over my following four decades as a pediatrician.

It was in this lab course that I learned about transfusion reactions. Teaching the enigmas of blood seemed particularly dear to The Turnip, perhaps because he was also the head of the blood bank that served the university hospital system. He regularly participated in the decisions which might lead to middle-of-the-night blood transfusions and was famous for his querulous questioning about the indications for a transfusion. It was the desperate ER and OR residents of these interrogatories who gave him his name. A generation of young doctors on the front lines had learned that getting a unit of blood from him when they were in dire straits was, well, like squeezing it from a turnip.

In those two semesters of laboratory medicine, we confronted three exams, then a comprehensive final in May. With only four chances to prove ourselves, each exam was critically important. Failing one exam was heart-stopping. Fail two, and your life was over. I don't remember much about the material covered by the first exam - but I will never forget learning of my personal outcome by the skipper's unique way of delivering the news.

My class sat at the slate counters in alphabetical order. The front was filled with inmates, last names beginning with "A." Balancing on the stools in the back were people like me, with names at the end of the alphabet. About two weeks after the first exam, The Turnip walked confidently to the lectern and announced that the following students would meet him in the back of the lab. With mic in hand, he read a list of names in alphabetical order and proceeded to the rear for the meeting. I had not been invited.

The meeting was brief. By the pallor of the returning dead men walking, I knew that the outcome of the exam had been disseminated and that I was seated among the grateful. I remember feeling relief and survivor's guilt, but I was not prepared for what came next: a private showdown with Dr. Bloodless.

I rarely had business with professors when my classmates first elected me class president a year earlier and I really don't remember any stressful presidential moments during my tenure that year. I had been re-elected when we returned the following fall to face the pesky *banditti* in the laboratory. Now, with a roomful of young adults in crisis, my status suddenly mattered. They badgered me in the cafeteria and vexed me privately before pharmacology class with the same imperative: *"You've got to do something!"*

But who was I? I had passed the first exam (glory to God) but I was hardly in a position to take on The Turnip. How would he receive an evaluation of his professorial style from a sophomore? I was merely another target, just as susceptible to a drive-by torpedo as the rest of them. I had enjoyed my relative obscurity among so many underclassmen. But now, *I* had to do something.

A few days after The Turnip fired his shot across the bow, I knocked on his office door and entered on command. The Turnip was bigger than me. Up close, he loomed, even from his desk chair. He seemed to know who I was, so I began: "My classmates asked me to speak to you about (*words – the right words*) their stress when they learned of the exam results. They felt like (*words, what words?*) it would help if those who failed could receive their results more confidentially."

The Turnip looked squarely up at me over his half rim reading glasses and spoke: "Is that all?"

"Yes, sir."

"I'll think about it."

"Thank you, sir."

About two weeks after the second exam, as we were adjusting our microscopes looking for who-knows-what, one whose name started with "W" through "Z" nudged me and indicated that I should look to the "A" and "B" section. The Turnip had slipped into the front of the lab with a clipboard and a smile (as I imagined.) He was scudding along the front row, checking the clipboard, breathing heavily (as I imagined), leaving wilting classmates in his wake and periodically pausing to whisper in the ear of the next loser. We who waited watched in horror as through the H – I - Js and R – S - Ts he navigated, leaving random derelicts swamped at their microscopes. Now it was the Ws turn.

I propped my microscope against my eyes to keep from falling off the stool. My eyepiece was fogged over because my eyeballs were sweating. The Turnip paused behind me, glanced at his clipboard and, like a specter on the deck of the *Flying Dutchman*, sailed silently past. Three years later, most of us were doctors and my professor's reputation remained unsullied. Blood is not easily squeezed from a turnip.

I tell this tale from medical school in 1968 to introduce my subject of how I had first learned student survival skills a few years earlier as a cadet under the severe eye of the Greatest Generation at The Citadel. From childhood, I knew about the college because the main gate was a few blocks from my grandparents' home in Charleston. When I visited at their house, I could hear the bugle calls in the quiet of late evenings and early mornings. Cannon fire and cheering from the football stadium would add spice to the sound track that put me to sleep on Friday nights in the fall.

I was ten years-old when General Mark Clark, one of the famous Generals of the wars in Europe and Korea, became the new President of The Citadel in 1954. I remember this history because I walked up to him after his first presidential review on the parade ground, introduced myself, congratulated him, and shook his hand. As a veteran navy brat, I was familiar with marching bands and uniforms and had shaken hands with officers before. I thought The Citadel was just another military base and that the General would be glad to meet me.

In those days, I dreamed I would be an artist when I grew up. As a high school senior, my application was accepted in two prominent schools of fine arts. But when I was actually deciding my future course of study, I had also been accepted at The Citadel. My older brother was beginning his junior year as a cadet there and my father had commented that a Bachelor of Science Degree would be more valuable than art training. I admired my big brother and it was my policy to listen to my father. So in the fall of 1962, I followed my dad's wisdom and my big brother's example.

My first day as a Citadel freshman in 1962 was a blur of numbing noise and confusion on the concrete quadrangle of the barracks. Along with endless instructions, quick marches here and there - and more noise - I was told of a manual of regulations which I would find in my room. Eventually I reached my room and as I closed the heavy wooden door that separated me from the chaos on the quad, I noticed a little blue book suspended from a hook. It had a liturgical look, like holy writ from Moses. In it was the Law that I had been told to learn, love and live. The title page read:

REGULATIONS
FOR THE
INTERIOR DISCIPLINE
AND POLICE OF THE
CORPS OF CADETS
OF
THE CITADEL

The Citadel Code illuminated page three. It was a set of ideals "earnestly commended to all cadets" by Mark W. Clark, President. There followed then a table of contents and an order signed by the adjutant. It informed that, concerning the little book, "each cadet will keep it in good condition, subject to inspection at all times" and more ominously, "ignorance of orders or regulations is not a valid excuse for failure to obey them." Concluding this introduction was a challenging definition of "discipline" by the French General who won his part of WWI:

DISCIPLINE

To be disciplined does not mean either that one executes orders received only in such measure as seems proper or possible, but it means that one enters freely into the thought and aims of the chief who has ordered, and that one takes every possible means to satisfy him. The first condition to obeying is, therefore, to visualize all the order received and nothing else, then to find the means of complying with it, irrespective of personal opinions, difficulties or obstacles. MARSHAL FOCH

I knew that Marshal Foch was saying something important, but that first day was not a time for reflection. "Entering freely into the thought and aims of the chief who ordered" was, for sure, beyond my capacity that day. I don't remember reading the entire *Blue Book*, but my corporal "chief," a junior second classman, had ordered me to do so and I must have. I do remember signing my name to a document a few weeks later certifying that I had read and understood the book, thereby complying with it:

5

16. – CONDUCT

16.02. FAMILUARIZATION WITH REGULATIONS: At the beginning of each semester, all cadets will be instructed in Rules and Regulations including Orders and Memoranda governing the conduct of cadets. Company Commanders will submit a certificate stating that all members of their organization and attached staff, where applicable, have read the Blue Book on or before 15 October.

Signing that I had read the book was the equivalent of officially agreeing that the Bill of Rights no longer applied to me. *The Blue Book of 1960* became my guide to four years of college life, what there would be of it. But in my days as a cadet, reading it was another command to obey "irrespective of personal opinions, difficulties or obstacles" (ref., the quotation from Marshal Foch.)

I occupied various rooms in Number 3 barracks over the years. But the little book was on the door of every barracks room, so it never ceased nagging me. *The Blue Book of 1960* was there when I rose with *Reveille* and tucked in at *Taps*. Even as a senior cadet, trying to live by the book (and often failing) was as physiological for me as breathing the secondhand cigarette smoke from various roommates.

Many years after graduating from The Citadel, I spotted a familiar little book with a blue paper cover in an estate sale. It never occurred to me that someone would take a *Blue Book* out of a barracks room, much less, offer it for sale.

So with a clear conscience, I satisfied the heirs and in the quiet of my life as a retired pediatrician, I reread the letter from the adjutant. In it was the not-so-subtle threat that my ignorance of regulations would not excuse my failures. Then the Colonel concluded his General Order No. 163 with a final instruction:

5. The spirit of these regulations will govern in all cases.

As I write these words, I realize that my life was radically affected by my usually earnest intent in those days to keep the spirit of *The Blue Book*, even as I also struggled to keep my sense of humor. Now in my geezerhood, I own a *Blue Book* and can read it as I did in the '60s. But today it is for amusement and for enjoying the serenity of having no heavy-breathing authority figure requiring my signature.

Academic Year 1962-1963

The status of a "cadet recruit" was zero. This was made clear from the moment the training cadre, the ranking cadets who were two or three years older and wiser, began organizing us on the quad that first morning. A few months earlier, we were big-deal, college-bound high school seniors. Now we were hapless nothings of the M Company recruit platoon, trying to appear soldierly in sorry-looking surplus army fatigues.

1. – THE CHARACTER OF THE COLLEGE

1.02. GUIDING PRINCIPLES:

b. Cleanliness: A cadet will be clean in the most exacting sense of the word. His hair must be short, face clean shaven and his body and clothes meticulously clean at all times. His equipment, furniture, room and every article and place for which he is responsible will be kept clean and tidy.

When our ranks formed, we were each issued a laundry bag and advised to stay in step as our sergeant marched us across the parade ground to Mark Clark Hall, the activities building. I followed the disordered and confused as they shuffled along until it was my turn in the barber chair. The man placed a shroud over most of me and airily inquired, "A little off the side?"

"Yes, sir," I replied.

His electric clippers, set on fully automatic, strafed all of my hair lifeless to the floor in a moment. "Next," he called, and I was gone.

I joined another line in the tailor shop, submitted to certain intimate measurements, and began filling my laundry bag with items of what comprised different uniforms. Then to the book store for a selection of texts, and to the armory, where I signed for a Garand M1 rifle. Eventually back on the quad, we were instructed in uniform-change drills and dismissed to begin the practices of the drill.

The purpose of uniform-change drill was to master dressing quickly. It was racing to our rooms, desperate offs-and-ons, then breathlessly realigning on the quadrangle. The next uniform might involve raincoats, athletic shorts or gray nasties, our duty uniform for classes and routine campus activities.

In private, metal stays, like straightened paperclips, had to be set precisely in the gray shirt collars and buckles had to be set to match the gig (the imaginary center line from your chin to your crotch). When we were gathered again, we learned and practiced the art of tucking in our long sleeve shirts and helping each other with shirt tucks, a somewhat odd ritual peculiar to knobs. With the assistance of the knob behind, the shirt of the knob ahead was stretched taught so that the back was entirely flat. During uniform drills, our rooms became dumps, mistakes happened and prices were paid. But we were learning efficiency and accuracy, skills that became life-saving at the time.

We were also learning push-ups and practicing squad drill in fatigues twice a day in the heat without canteens. To prevent hyponatremia, we were periodically directed to swallow a salt tablet. (To prevent dehydration was not a consideration.) When we eventually marched back to the barracks, the cadre proved that we were well-hydrated by producing fresh sweat from more push-ups and running us up and down the stairs.

Back in my room, I worked on making my shoes and the metal elements of my uniform shine. The pungent smells of brass polish and shoe wax, along with the odor of wet clothes suffused the atmosphere when I faced straightening up the place. Each piece of laundry, from tee shirts to socks, had to be folded and displayed. The rifle had to be cleaned before it was placed on the special, built-in shelf braced on the bookcase. There could be no dust or dirt anywhere and in the end, there could be no trash in the trash can. It would be months before I was efficiently living my life by the principle of "clean and tidy," as directed by *The Blue Book*. But this was the first day of what was known later as "Hell Week."

The Citadel Code "earnestly commended to all cadets": To cultivate dignity, poise, affability and a quiet and firm demeanor.
– Mark W. Clark, President

One of the first critical skills I learned as a cadet recruit was how to maintain a "firm demeanor," although I don't recall that the practice of achieving a deliberate absence of facial expression was called anything particularly. With a firm demeanor, I corrected errors, dismissed contrary emotions, and carried on.

I was one of eight or ten freshmen who formed a squad in the fourth class platoon of M Company. We were receiving drill instruction in the heat of that first day and we looked ridiculous. The short guys wore olive green fatigue pants that were too long and so, rolled up; the skinny guys also looked ridiculous in their OG trash bags. After an hour, I had learned about "attention," "right shoulder arms," and "order arms." Then we were learning how to move from here to there. It was this, it was that – back and forth, then doing it again. At some point, I was at the end of the line when a command produced a train wreck.

In that moment, somebody was going this way, somebody that way, somebody stopping, and somebody tripping. From the caboose, I saw it all as the train went off the rails. That was when I lost what firm demeanor

I had been practicing and worse, I laughed. Laughing, I then learned, was the actual disaster. In the dark of my room, hopeless hours later, I heard the wrought iron gates of the barracks shut as *Taps* sounded. *Remember*, I told myself, *it's not funny. No expression. No laughing. Firm demeanor.*

Photograph from the author's collection

Squad Drill on the Parade Ground in September of 1962

This is an unpublished image which the photographer encouraged me to purchase. He was a senior capo in the cadre who had a wife to support. He told me that by buying the photo, I was not only preserving a cherished memory for myself, but also I was contributing to the welfare of the family. His enterprise was against regulations, but as I handed over my cash, I felt like I was becoming a wise guy and a part of La Cosa Nostra.

After Friday practice parade, a truce was called. Scattered hours on the weekends were for "general leave" for cadets who qualified. It was possible (not necessarily probable) that in these hours a cadet could pass through the main gate of the campus and come up for air at the King Street-Citadel bus stop. But the anonymous bugler was always waiting on weekend evenings, eager to blow away illusions of peace and herald again the foreboding reality.

I stayed in my room that first Friday evening, furiously spinning my wheels in an effort to shine and clean an endless sort of stuff that required shining and cleaning. I did make a break for it on Saturday evening, walking the few blocks to my grandparents' home to take a nap. In the attic near my bed were the folded uniforms of my uncle who had been a cadet thirty years before. It seemed like no more than a moment had passed before my grandmother called to me that it was time to go. I took one last glance in the mirror by the front door as I left to consider: *Hat straight, gig straight, firm demeanor.*

Resting in security for a little while exacerbated my dread as I reentered the barracks. I lived up on the 3rd division and had a long way to go before I reached the relative safety of my room. The 1st division gallery was dark and empty when I squared the corner from the sally port. It looked like a creepy alley in a horror movie that compels you to involuntarily call out with everyone else, "Don't go there!" I should have listened to the audience as their pupils dilated and they spilled their popcorn.

I was moving at the required 120 steps per minute ("tooling") and approaching the stairwell when a sepulchral voice I recognized called out from the shadows, "HALT!" I slammed on the brakes and entered the skid that would eventually stop all the momentum. In that same moment, I was struck on the back of my head by some UFO. A second later, I became aware of hot breath at my ear.

Unsurprisingly, I had failed again and briefly suffered the consequences of correction before I was commanded to proceed. I never saw my inquisitor in the darkness, but I had two junior corporals who were devoted to my improvement. One was very scary, the other less so. The voice and the breath belonged to Mister Veryscary.

When I finally crawled into the upper bunk in my room, I faced a fitful night of listening to the old, toothless lion occasionally roar from his cage in the Hampton Park Zoo, less than a mile away. A few hours later, my alarm clock buzzed me into action. I had to prepare for Sunday *First Call* and *Reveille.*

I was momentarily delayed in getting up from my bunk because the pillow was stuck to my head. As I pealed it away, I realized that the glue was my own blood: *I must have a cut on my head.* For a moment, I considered the UFO of the evening before, then cleaned the unseen gore as best I could.

A little later, I was at attention in breakfast formation when my corporal approached me. "West," he hissed, "give me permission to lift your hat."

That was a proper request, by the book. "Yes, sir," I replied.

I felt him move my hat from behind, and replace it. Then he sizzled in my ear, "Last night, you broke my hat brass." So that was the UFO! His black garrison hat was the flying saucer and it was the two-inch brass palmetto insignia on the crown that rendered me *hors de combat*, as Marshal Foch might have said.

I don't remember my corporal requiring me to speak. I had been severely warned not to speak to anyone in authority unless directly instructed to do so. It would have been best not to have spoken. Maybe it was in my fevered dreams or a memory of what my mother taught me as a little boy…but it seems like I said, "I'm sorry for breaking your hat brass, sir."

40. – RIGHTS OF REDRESS

40.01. SUBMISSION OF COMPLAINT: If any cadet shall consider himself wronged by another cadet or by any officer of the college, he may submit a complaint through the Commandant of Cadets.

I did not report to the Commandant that I had been wronged and the incident apparently evaporated into the oblivion I myself longed to enter. It is true, though, that my corporal never – never – corrected me personally again.

With the passage of time, I reviewed what I had learned those first few days:

- A firm demeanor was undefined, but essential for survival.
- Even though the rules regulating a firm demeanor were not in *The Blue Book*, nothing was funny and no fear or pain was allowed.
- Though registering a complaint with the Commandant might be a theoretical possibility by the book, not doing so was smarter and the code of *omerta* would help assure another dawn for me.

On the last evening of the first week, I was introduced to bracing while standing in a barracks corner room, a living space for four. That evening, the room was occupied by more than fifty. The training cadre grandly guarded the windows, thereby owning half of the standing space and blocking whatever hope remained for fresh air. I shared my acreage across the room between the bunks with the forty-some freshmen of M Company who were no longer under the mistaken impression that we had been accepted at the Military College of South Carolina.

One of our tormentors was standing on a table in an extreme posture of military "attention." He was the lone sophomore of the cadre, barely four months beyond his own freshman year. Now he held the lofty status of "company clerk" and in this moment, he served as the model for our instruction.

A cadre officer pointed out details: His head was erect, his eyes were straight ahead, and his face without expression. His chin was severely compressed against his throat and his shoulders were thrust back and down. His chest was lifted and thrust forward as his spine remained straight; his abdomen was tensely drawn inward. His arms were rigidly alongside, elbows tucked in, and on each side, his thumb and index finger aligned with the respective pant seam. His butt was rolled forward, his knees were together and slightly flexed, his heels joined and his feet fanned apart at 45 degrees.

Knowledge of bracing was undoubtedly another life-saving piece of information for me, so I tried to process this new idea of how to stand (a skill I thought I had mastered some years previously.) But bracing was only one of countless critical secrets of cadet life which had pummeled me in the past few days like a hail storm. I supposed we would soon be practicing how to stand, just as we were already practicing how to speak correctly and how to sit at a dinner table (also skills I thought I knew already.)

I could hear the officer describe bracing from my place along the back wall. But what I could actually see was little more than the closely shaved nape of the knob in whose neck my nose was embedded. I believe that was when I first became aware of the odor of confined freshmen: it was distinctly noisome whenever we gathered in a closed area. It was the smell of fear.

The instruction on bracing was abruptly suspended when the room door crashed open and a half dozen men three years older than most of us shouldered their way to the front. These gangbangers looked dark and mean. Above all, they were clearly in charge.

Our cadre introduced them as the officers of the battalion staff. We were to look at them carefully as their names and exalted positions were heralded. When we next encountered them, we would be expected to know the identity of each and address each specifically by name (that is, "Sir, Mister..., sir") when necessary. From the back of the room, I saw these thugs only by peripheral vision as they swept past me, their garrison hat bills pulled low on their faces. The formal introductions were of no practical help because as I looked, I simply became further acquainted with the sweaty, stubby scalp in front of me.

As dramatically as the Great Ones had come, they vanished. Our first sergeant then dismissed us to our rooms with the parting thought that tonight the plebe system would officially be in effect and we would be expected on the quadrangle shortly in bathrobes. A little later I was standing in formation on the darkened barracks quadrangle. In the dusk and silence, low murmurs and occasional, sinister snickers from the corner stairwell were accented by flickers of cigarette lighters casting looming shadows up dark, hard walls. The gangstas were gathering.

The quiet was eventually broken by the big wrought iron gates creaking and groaning, then clanking shut. The chain rattled as it was pulled across the secured gates. The exaggerated click of the padlock snap added a certain finality. I knew then that the lock was not to keep interlopers out – it was to keep me in.

With a much louder, amplified click, the barracks P.A. opened. A melancholy rendition of "*Home, Sweet Home*" echoed across the quad and a disembodied voice spoke: "This is the Regimental Commander. The Plebe System for 1962-63 is now in effect." That was the night that I was reintroduced to the battalion staff, learned all about bracing, and determined that I would stay to see what came next.

I recall only a small part of those first seven days which were known then as "Knob Week." But I remember that the barracks was a combat zone, survival was the priority, and adrenaline was my nourishment. Perhaps the most critical lesson I had learned was that emotions and attitudes were former luxuries. They may not be mentioned in the book, but along with most other things, they were forbidden. In the days that followed, if there was any relief, it was in the solitude of my room with my *Blue Book.*

Social details of those days also run together. My first roommate disappeared soon after we met and I cannot remember his name now. Neither can I remember the name of the next one - he, also, was soon gone. Another roommate was a jock on "athletic orders." He was putting in his hours with sports training and so was missing part of the barracks ordeal. I think he transferred out or resigned.

My one memorable roommate was so regularly in trouble that I didn't see much of him either. Particulary, I remember him after *Taps* one evening. In the quiet of the barracks, he could be heard echoing loudly into one of the big corrugated cans that stood guard at the corner of each gallery stairwell: "Sir, Mr. Trashcan, sir, I apologize for touching you, sir."

16. – CONDUCT

16.04. GENERAL RULES GOVERNING CONDUCT:

q. Profane, impure or improper language is prohibited.

From the beginning, I was under the impression that the rules in my *Blue Book* apparently did not apply to the upper class training cadre. Freshmen were officially called "cadet recruits" at the start. Unofficially we were "knobs" or "smacks" at best. Far more descriptive nouns, along with colorful adjectives, were always percolating and liberally served when corrections were necessary. (In those first weeks, such corrections were moment to moment.)

2. – HAZING

2.02. HAZING DEFINED: Hazing is any unauthorized assumption of authority by one cadet over another whereby the latter shall or may suffer any cruelty, indignity, or oppression, or the deprivation of any right, privilege or advantage to which he shall be legally entitled.

Closely scheduled formations on the quad and drills on the parade ground offered seamless opportunity for public humiliation, usually associated with pushups and/or running on the stairs. Evening "sweat parties" in the closed down and steamed up shower rooms were especially instructive. Such group encounters with local law enforcement would often be followed by further degradation in private.

One morning my effort at shaving apparently rendered more of a French *dadhi* style then the expected cue ball chin. The result was noise and push-ups on the quadrangle then later, a remedial dry shave in my room, my head being inside the darkness of the metal bucket which served as my trash can. Band-Aids then frustrated me for several more days in fully satisfying the requirement to be clean-shaven.

A parallel incident drew me into a closer relationship with my rifle, (which I affectionately dubbed, "my rifle.") The incident began as my squad was standing at parade rest. My legs were separated and my right arm was extended, thrusting my rifle barrel forward with the rifle butt tipped and grounded beside my shoe. If you were to try this, you would find that you can only enclose the upper fore stock of your rifle with your thumb and index finger. Your other fingertips are then touching the fore stock but not really locking it in place.

I was unaware of this tenuous grip until my alert sergeant kicked the stock forward from behind me. Dropping your rifle is barely less offensive than dropping the American flag, for which I believe summary execution is imposed. For this lesser offense, I was required to sleep with my rifle that night. Many years passed before I realized *The Blue Book of 1960* warned cadets against firearms in their rooms:

9. – BARRACKS ADMINISTRATION

9.12. FIREARMS, AMMUNITION AND EXPLOSIVES: No cadet shall have in his possession in barracks any fire arms, ammunition, explosive material of any kind or privately owned firearms. Any cadet having knowledge of any unauthorized fire arms, ammunition, or explosives will report the fact to the Commandant of Cadets without delay.

If I was true to the book in those days, I would have reported to the Commandant the fact that there was a firearm in my room – worse, in my bed. My failure though, pales when compared to my confusion from an equally important expectation of the Commandant:

36. - PROPERTY

36.05. RIFLE: Cadets not armed with the sword will draw and care for a rifle.

I was just a knob without a sword and I had a firearm in my room. Did the Commandant know this? Did the upper class live by revelation from a superior *Blue Book*? Should I request permission to ask a question of my tormentors? That last question was a thing too great for me to contemplate – and too many conflicting ideas mocked me from every side. So I went with the sergeant's recommendation and kept my mouth shut. That's how my rifle and I became better acquainted.

2. – HAZING

2.05. VISITING ROOMS: No upper classman *(sic)* will visit the room of a fourth classman except in the execution of an official duty.

A few days later, my second Sunday afternoon as a cadet, knob week was over and the plebe system for the class of '66 was underway. Meanwhile, the rest of the corps had returned for the academic year. The barracks were quiet and I was alone in my room when the toggle on my door clicked. An unseen presence entered. As I had been taught, I "popped" to attention, looking straight ahead. The presence approached and spoke: "Ed – it's just me."

It was my big brother, a junior in C Company – the guy who used to be my roommate in our family of four boys. His was the first kindly voice I had heard since I could no longer remember when. I glanced over toward him, my eyes filled with tears. He looked oddly at me and said, "Whatever you do, don't cry." By the book, my brother's visit was not proper. In that moment, I differed – I guess he did, too.

2. – HAZING

2.04. ORDERING A CADET TO REPORT: Except as specifically prescribed in the subparagraphs which follow, no cadet shall order another to any room for correction, instruction, bracing or for any purpose whatsoever.

It is almost unbelievable, but I considered almost none of the adverse events in the barracks that directly involved me to be "hazing." One of the moments I remember thinking to myself, *this is hazing*, was when I was in my sergeant's room "sitting on the green stool." The green stool was a sturdy wooden shoe box with a hinged top that stood about a foot off the floor. There was one in each room and it contained all of the items used to shine and polish.

Sitting on the green stool did not actually involve "sitting." A knob would first stand on the shoe box so that he could then assume a deep squat. As his knees were folding down into the squat, a helpful upperclassman would place a broom handle behind the knees. At this point, the knob was actually supported only by his toes on the top of the box.

The freshman would then extend his arms together, straight forward with hands facing downward. Now in a deep squat, arms extended and otherwise bracing his body, and with the broom locked behind his knees, the helpful assistant would then place a rifle across the knob's extended wrists.

In my experience, sitting on the green stool was probably hazing – but it really wasn't so bad. The broom behind my knees soon cut off the circulation to my lower legs and I would find relief in falling off the box. Of course, there was an additional price to pay for the rifle hitting the floor.

The Citadel Code "earnestly commended to all cadets": To face difficulties with courage and fortitude and not to complain or be discouraged. – Mark W. Clark, President

I was trapped in the straits of formal education for about twenty-five of my years on the planet. I learned to be a reliable student in those years, but I usually didn't enjoy being a student - especially in February. My Februaries went backwards when I was in school. Then long, dreary Februaries continued throughout my forty years as a pediatrician. In pediatrics, February was always the month of midnight fevers and mocking sunrises, viewed from ER ambulance bays after hospital all-nighters.

But my longest February was in 1963 when I was a freshman at The Citadel. That February I was ready to concede. I had crawled across the finish line of my first semester with little hope for the next bleak months. We had lost at least one in four of the M Company knobs of September and I had begun preliminary correspondence with admissions clerks of other colleges.

Above Illustrations (The) Shako, Spring, 1964

The downhill slide had begun in October when I passed out in a Friday parade formation. The doctor at the infirmary observed that I was the color of a cheddar cheese cracker. He diagnosed hepatitis. I was transferred to the Charleston Naval Hospital where needle sticks eventually drained away the cheddar along with most of my blood, leaving me the color of a saltine. There exists a black-and-white photograph of me a month later and even without the colors, I truly do look terminal.

When I returned from the naval hospital, I convalesced in the infirmary and was excused from military duty (XMD) over the next two months. I had little appetite, felt miserable most of the time, and slept. Meanwhile, I developed a working relationship with the doctor (officially known as the "Surgeon.")

I knew as I languished in the infirmary that I had an opportunity to succeed in academics. I also knew that my classmates were learning survival skills that would be yet waiting for me to learn. I was aware of the struggles of my classmates in the company. But unless we incidentally shared class room time, I was detached from them socially. I dropped my German modern language course because of the missed classwork that occurred during my hospitalization off campus. But otherwise, since there was nothing else to do, I usually made classes and studied.

After Christmas furlough, then semester break, I returned to the barracks in a weakened condition. Along with losing my jaundice and anemia, I had also lost about twenty pounds - weight I really couldn't afford to lose. So I was still XMD by the surgeon's order, sharing an alcove room on a corner of the 3rd division with a new roommate.

My roommate was a quiet guy whose own roomie did not return the second semester. Pragmatically, he was my lifesaver. He had spent his first semester learning how to make it and with his help, I learned the ropes quickly. The shortcuts he taught me saved critical minutes in a day and they are probably still used today by successful knobs. I will not develop this part of the story in detail for the sake of those who still must survive their freshman year through the secrets being preserved. My hope is that they will learn the tricks quickly enough.

Because my medical status was XMD in those first days of return, I did not have to brace or march, so in the barracks and formations, I felt like a spectator of a genocide. It seemed bizarre and unethical that I should be no more than a voyeur as my classmates suffered. When I read *The Blue Book* on the subject of XMD, I thought I found a better way:

41. - SERVICES

41.07. MEDICAL SERVICE:

b. Status of cadet marked Excused Military Duty

(1) A cadet marked "XMD" will not be required to perform military duty or march in ranks. He will meet all company formations and after report of absentees has been received by the 1st Sergeant he will fall out, report to his company or detachment commander, and proceed alone to the place of duty, except that he will not be required to attend close order drill or parades.

The regulation held that an XMD cadet was not required to participate in the particularly stressful part of knob barracks life. But maybe I could voluntarily participate and use my XMD status only when I thought it was necessary. So with fear and trembling, I requested a word with the 1st Sergeant. The result was an informal and undocumented amendment to the intention of the regulation. The 1st Sergeant would officially carry me on reports as "XMD" as I joined my classmates to the extent that I could. He would trust my judgment on the question of participation – and I had better be correct! I realize now that this decision placed him at risk for a charge of "poor judgment," should my health fail or should I double-cross him.

As a means of monitoring my condition and the wisdom of my participation in the barracks fourth class system, the 1st Sergeant assigned me to his table in the mess hall. This meant that I would learn critical lessons under his immediate scrutiny, three times a day. Forever. When classmates became aware of my status and this policy, they generally opined that I was doing better when I only had hepatitis.

Many of my fellow knobs had experienced the 1st Sergeant up close and personal in a routine they called the "7-7 shift." This time of fun required reporting to the corner room shared by the Company Commander and 1st Sergeant week days at 0700 hours and 1900 hours (7 a.m. and 7 p.m.) Various individually prescribed exercises would then be privately practiced for fifteen or twenty minutes as the Great Ones casually lived their lives in their rooms.

19. - DINING HALL

19.04. ORGANIZATION

a. Preparatory to entering the Dining Hall cadets will be assigned to table groups of fourteen cadets. Each fourteen man table will be divided evenly with the senior cadet designated as Carver seated at each end.

The tables in the mess hall were placed in pairs, end-to-end and aligned across the large rooms in rows by battalions. Each elongated double table was covered by a white table cloth which draped down to the knees of those seated. At each table end sat the mess carver, a ranking cadet, most often a senior. One or two upperclassmen sat closest to him for convenient conversation; a sophomore or two might be seated beside these. Knobs were concentrated in the center area of the two conjoined mess tables, the freshmen focused on serving the men of their respective messes.

Dining in the mess hall was for others – knobs were too busy to eat. At least this was the case on the mess of the 1st Sergeant. I was one of two or three freshman who by continuous surveillance, assured that there was always milk – or sweet tea, or coffee. There was always the next serving of potatoes or turnips; there was always butter, salt, cream and sugar.

On mess, I remained continuously at an exaggerated state of attention. I sat on the front few inches of my chair as I performed my duties under the lifeless eye of the 1st Sergeant. Should I find a moment to serve myself some beans, I would begin this process (with doubtful hope of success) by a spoken request: "Sir, Mr..., sir, would you or any of the other gentlemen care for more beans?" If the answer was negative, I would place a spoonful of beans on my plate. Under the circumstances, I mostly gave up on the idea of eating at mess. Two glazed doughnuts and a cup of coffee at Mark Clark Hall usually provided most of my fuel.

I was regularly required to have an "interesting fact" to contribute to the upper class table talk when it suited them. The facts I offered were always new information and were scrutinized by unspecified standards. I quickly learned that what I thought was new and interesting did not necessarily engage the 1st Sergeant. So I listened more to his table conversations and tailored my facts to match his taste.

19. - DINING HALL

19.07. GENERAL RULES IN DINING HALL:

c. The Carver is responsible that gentlemanly and orderly conduct is maintained and that dining hall regulations are enforced.

f. The recitation by Fourth Classmen in a loud voice is expressly prohibited.

The mess hall was noisy. The general cacophony interfered in communication down the table length, so more volume was necessary. The sense was being in a room full of people shouting at each other. Paradoxically, in the background was the calming ebb and flow of recorded beach music. But even *Louie Louie* was blown away by the full-volume expression of the 1st Sergeant: "I CAN'T HEAR YOU, KNOB!" More noise would follow.

When I made a mistake (common, initially), I usually was rewarded with the 1st Sergeant's wrath. By my peripheral vision, I would become aware of his focused glare. By reflex, I learned to brace in preparation for his correction which was sure to come. Sometimes he would rise up and in a moment be at my ear with a sizzling piece of insight, advice or direction. Before long, I was on his 7-7 shift.

On weekday mornings, we were usually returning to the barracks from breakfast just before 7 o'clock (0700 hours) This gave me time to tool up to the 1st Sergeant's room and bang twice on his door (as was the custom.) An invitation to "drive in" resulted.

I don't remember the first moment of my reporting for 7-7 shift; neither do I remember subsequent moments specifically. I do remember that reporting at 0700 hours and again at 1900 hours was what I did for those winter weeks that semester. I also remember enjoying the toasty warmth of my 1st Sergeant's room, particularly because of what I usually did during the visit. I learned the routine quickly:

When I entered his room, he often didn't even look up at me. I proceeded directly to the exposed iron wall radiator and assumed a brace with my back to the wall, about 6-inches off the radiator. Then leaning stiffly straight backwards on my heels, I stabilized my balance with the rear of my head against the wall and the rest of me exposed over the radiator. I completed the required minutes of slow roasting in silence until he told me to get lost - which I did.

Allowing for interrupted travel on the galleries and stairs, I probably lost about 45 minutes a day of unscheduled time while I was on the 7-7 shift. Much more time-consuming were the routines my roommate and I practiced caring for the personal demands of the three seniors who lived in the corner room beside us. They were funny and harmless; they could be gross sometimes.

2. – HAZING

2.03. PERSONAL SERVICES: Fourth classmen will not be detailed nor will they be permitted to perform any services for an upper classman such as opening or closing windows or doors of rooms, sweeping rooms, handling beds or bedding, cleaning equipment, etc. A violation of this paragraph is an act of hazing.

My relationship with our seniors was basically "at ease" but always with a "sir" in conversation. My roomie and I shined their shoes and brass, ran errands, picked up laundry, made beds, and repeatedly swept and dusted their room. Weekly formal inspections took more time on Friday nights during general leave. The tasks were, of course, in addition to tending to our own military upkeep and academic studies.

Somewhat unique in my case was a duty a senior living alone in an upper division room required. He knew he was heading for medical school after graduation and was almost always studying when I was around him. My role in his life occurred only on cold mornings before *Reveille* when I would scurry down to the latrine and take a seat. About ten minutes later, I would hear him at the entrance: "West, you in here, boy?"

"Yes, sir," I would reply cheerily.

"Where you at, boy?" he would ask.

"Sir, I'm down here on the last pot, sir," I would say.

He would then appear at the stall with his newspaper and say, "Get out of here, boy."

The seat would be warmed to his satisfaction and I would unobtrusively evacuate.

My future-doctor senior was a little quirky but not dangerous to knobs. My squad sergeant, on the other hand, was loathsome for sure. He didn't have to say he hated me for me to come to that conclusion. He moved me toward maturity in the casual manner of a cat pawing at a cornered cockroach, confident that only one of the two would be walking away.

The sergeant was a senior. I had heard that he was in academic limbo and might not graduate. I knew that he had a girlfriend and that the beast in him was soothed by the husky voice of Julie London, seducing him from a phonograph record. I became aware of these details of his life because I spent so much time in the shadows of his little room up on the 4th division where he lived alone (except for his girl's picture and Julie's voice crying him a river.) Those times in his room I would rather not recall. It was hazing, but I considered it normal.

So, I felt like I was sinking fast in the depths of February. I began to consider alternatives to a Citadel diploma. I actually applied to some other colleges and told my parents my thoughts. They were my most faithful supporters and advised me to do what seemed best. I know they had their opinions, but they kept them within their private conversation. Still, I held one ace that I had not yet played and from my radio, Maurice Williams and the Zodiacs were encouraging me to *Stay*.

Above Illustrations (*The) Shako*, Spring, 1964

In my first weeks as a knob, I had learned that not everyone was to be saluted. One person I mistakenly saluted because he had gold stars on his dress-uniform collar. (Surely, if ANY one should be saluted, it would be someone with gold stars on his collar!) Turns out, not so much. Gold stars were for academic achievement, not for signifying rank. Even a freshman might be wearing "gold stars" after the first semester, although failure and withdrawal from the school was far more likely. Gold stars had a mystique about them – unattainable, like Julie London.

Somehow, I did well in my studies my first semester. When I returned to the barracks after the semester furlough, I knew that my grades had qualified me for gold stars. But no one told me where to go to get them. Meanwhile, dreary February routines of inspections, parades and daily mess formations before the sun came up and then, after it went down, were endured with dread on the quadrangle. Repeatedly I would brace in formation as my squad sergeant breathed into my ear his appraisal of my failure as a human being. In moments of solitude in ranks, my forlorn hope was invisibility.

On one particular February Friday afternoon, I was in full dress uniform in the third platoon at the back of the company. This location was barely preferable to being in one of the other two platoons, where a knob was more likely to be evaluated by someone as august as the company commander. I could not see much beyond all the shakos between me and the action in the front. But I could see the blue guidon pennant moving as commands were barked and I could see the brilliant black feathers of the cadet officers' plumes fluttering above the other shako pom poms.

In this moment, I was following the routine commands and tentatively appreciating my anonymity when, to my horror, I heard my name called out from the front. Now what? In five months, I had never been publicly singled out from the front of the company.

"West – get up to the front of the company!" hissed my squad sergeant.

What did that mean? How do you get up to the front of the company? No one had ever told me there was even the possibility of such a military maneuver, much less how to accomplish it. We were in full dress uniforms – breastplates, white gloves, rifles – the works. I could hear the band beckoning on the parade ground like the sirens of Ulysses. How do I get up to the front of the company from the third platoon?

My helpful squad sergeant made his contribution to my solution: "Get up to the front of the company, you stupid, blinkety-blankety-blank-anatomical parts-blank." In the grandeur of military tradition, my only hope was to advance. For sure, I was a dead man where I was. Then I recalled what the Marshal said:

DISCIPLINE

To be disciplined does not mean either that one executes orders received only in such measure as seems proper or possible, but it means that one enters freely into the thought and aims of the chief who has ordered, and that one takes every possible means to satisfy him. The first condition to obeying is, therefore, to visualize all the order received and nothing else, then to find the means of complying with it, irrespective of personal opinions, difficulties or obstacles. MARSHAL FOCH

The order received was "Get up to the front of the company!" To follow the marshal's advice and please my chief, I knew what I had to do.

There is a prescribed manner for an individual in ranks to approach the front of the unit. For me, it would have entailed an about-face, right-face, port-arms and then forward-march to the end of the squad. At the far end of the squad, I would smartly cut on the left flank of the company in a column-right, and then again a column-right at the forward corner of the first platoon. Concluding, I would have come to a halt in the front of the officers, faced them, and reported smartly with a rifle salute.

I didn't know this on the only occasion I needed the information. But I knew what I had to do. So I gathered my rifle and began to wander through the ranks of the two platoons ahead of me. ("Excuse me, sir; excuse me, sir...") As the men of the forward platoons laughed, hooted and cursed, my squad sergeant sounded as though he were about to suffer a fatal vascular event. His volume and eloquence rose to meet the emergency as he speculated on my birthright and exquisitely defined the nature of my natal origins, along with my cranial contents, which apparently were awkwardly displaced below my white waist belt.

Somewhere during my sojourn within the first platoon, it occurred to me: This must be when I get my gold stars. My sergeant is on the verge of flunking out and he's calling me an idiot. I am dead meat after parade today – but this is funny. I kept my firm demeanor, as I had been trained. But only I knew how much I was enjoying the moment as I received my gold stars. I had played my ace and won the hand.

Regaining my sense of humor was a game-changer that dark February afternoon. I had hope again. I grimly recommitted to success and looked for ways to cope other than simply despairing. It wasn't the stars that gave me hope – it was the joy of overcoming. I knew for sure I was going to make it.

Over the next weeks, I became reacquainted with my artist's muse. I also began to draw cartoons of my life and hard times for *The Shako*, the literary and humor magazine. In the fall, I had first seen a copy of *The Shako* which was produced by cadets three times a year and offered an outlet for personal expression. I especially was attracted to the magazine's tolerance for sketchy opinions in a highly authoritarian culture which oddly offered its official blessing to such overripe gas from underage Hemmingways. The editors were looking for fresh talent and I had experience in publications from high school days. So I made an effort, met some people, and became an artist on the magazine staff.

The next edition of *The Shako* was being prepared for a Corps Day deadline in March when I submitted my offerings. My primary job was to illustrate short stories submitted by cadets. But the fun was in producing cartoons. I had observed some truly unlikely truths in the past six months concerning how life was supposed to be compared to how life was in reality and I was ready to be heard.

The First Woman in My Life

This cartoon was my first contribution to The Shako. My mother was sending me a weekly check for five dollars and silently suffering at home on my behalf.

I THINK I'LL GIVE UP THE PLEBE SYSTEM FOR LENT.

Apprentice Artist on The Shako Staff

The mortar holding the Berlin Wall together was still drying when I first submitted my cartoons for The Shako and I sensed that I was trapped in the Eastern Sector. Meanwhile, barracks life had made me more coarse and cynical. As a knob, I had learned that daily survival was a function of my maintaining invisibility, so I signed my work for publication with the device referring to my company rather than with my name.

A development on campus gave me the inspiration for a cartoon which was to raise me up further than the stars. In the news was word that the British government had offered certain parts of a WW2 submarine to General Clark as a memento. *HMS Seraph* had provided him with underwater transportation to a dangerous shore in 1943 on a clandestine mission. Now the *Seraph* was about to be decommissioned and the Brits knew that General Clark enjoyed collecting used military hardware like tanks and torpedoes. His artifacts were deployed around campus and comprised what was reverently known to the cadets as the General's Army Surplus Store.

When leaving campus at the main gate one weekend, I had noticed that a concrete mammillary form had been constructed beside the library. It was about fifteen feet high and hollow. Arches permitted a person to enter it and peruse within, where there was mounted a periscope, raised through the top of the great tata.

I walked over to this odd half-of-an-upright-eggshell broaching the ground and peered through the periscope eyepiece. The magnified view was several hundred yards across the parade ground to Number 2 barracks.

From the tower, the Stars and Stripes were fluttering above and intruding into the view from behind the barracks was the towering, yellow brick chimney of the campus power plant. This seemed to align with the barracks parapet in a somewhat discordant manner. Yet it was a plausible part of the still life. The effect of the periscope view was of a large warship, steaming majestically on the calm green sea of the parade ground with a hot stack and unfurled colors. My muse interrupted the moment: It was a target!

Just like my father's submarine skipper used to do - I began considering the range, course, speed and angle on the bow.

I was concerned about my lowly knob status when I submitted my first set of cartoons, so I didn't sign my work. But the editors saw more than I did and gave me a whole page with a title. This was when I truly figured out how to sink Number 2 barracks. It was also the first of my featured contributions in subsequent issues which the editors had decided to title, "CID SCENES."

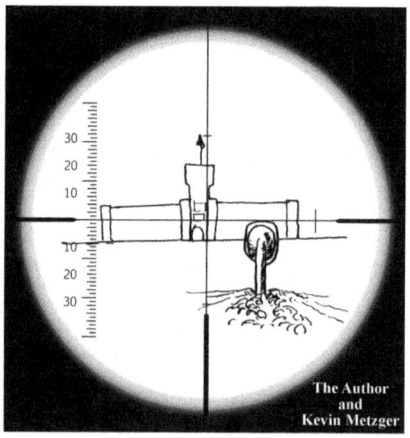

The Author
and
Kevin Metzger

CID SCENES

by ed west

1

5

2

6

3

7

4

8

(The) Shako,
Spring, 1963

16. – CONDUCT

16.04. GENERAL RULES GOVERNING CONDUCT:

k. Damage to property: Any cadet who shall wantonly or accidentally damage, destroy, or make away *(sic)* any public property connected with the college shall be charged with the cost of the property and punished according to the degree of the offense.

The result of my vision was my first significant contribution to *The Shako*: The Sinking of Number 2 Barracks. Not only did it briefly bring a modest notoriety with some of my classmates, it also taught me that the system was vulnerable to an attack of the pen. I had wantonly (if vicariously) destroyed public property connected with the college, sipped a cup of *schadenfreude*, and gotten away with it.

19. – DINING HALL

19.02. ORGANIZATION

e. The Carver is responsible that gentlemanly and orderly conduct is maintained and that dining hall regulations are enforced.

Adding to this new-found fun was an adventure in the mess hall. I was off the 7-7 shift, but still on the 1st Sergeant's mess and living on doughnuts. I had become so accomplished at serving and spouting facts at mess that corrections were much less frequent. Beyond this, the 1st Sergeant seemed more ready to engage me in conversation that was almost "normal." But as the tension lessened, a new risky mission was privately ordered: I was to slip under the table and squirt mustard on the shoes of his classmate, the mess carver sitting at the opposite end of the long table.

The Citadel Code "earnestly commended to all cadets": To perform every duty with fidelity and conscientiousness and to make DUTY my watchword. – Mark W. Clark, President

I was aware of the possibilities of disaster that came with this mission because some of my classmates had suffered for their failures. There was an unspoken agreement among the upperclassmen, however, to not hold a successful knob raider accountable. I accepted the odds, made DUTY my watchword, and prepared to slip under the table when the opportunity seemed ripe.

A moment occurred when the other mess was engaged enough to seem unaware of our half of the long table. I was seated four chairs away from the other mess carver when I slithered down and out of my chair with the mustard. Under the table cover, I assumed a crawl position among the legs and feet. Then, carefully avoided disturbing the cypress knees in the black water twilight and watching for alerted denizens, I reached with the mustard squeeze bottle past the last pair of legs and left my mark. As the level of noise from above continued without change in volume, I began spelunking backward out past the stalagmites and recovered my upright place at the table.

I was allowed to be excused from the table sooner than usual, so I missed the moment of reckoning on the other mess. With gold stars, credit for sinking Number 2 barracks, and success on my special ops mess mission, I was on a roll. Two years later I celebrated this modest victory in the context of a larger illustrated *Shako* article named "Status is..."

Status is getting your sergeants shoes under the table.

Status is catching him.

(The) Shako,
Fall, 1965

My sense of humor and perspective were recovering when word came that certain sophomore privates would be promoted to corporal.

15. – COMPANY ADMINISTRATION

15.01. DUTIES OF LEADERS:

i. The Company Clerk: The Company Clerk will assist the First Sergeant in the preparation of all company papers. He will serve only one interior guard tour each semester. He will not be excused from Saturday Morning Inspection.

In September of 1962, corporals were juniors. The only sophomores with military status were the company clerks (who were privates.) As a class, sophomores were universally considered by the upperclassmen to be knobs who could walk around with their chins out. This low opinion influenced the viewpoint of the freshmen who saw sophomores as annoying, prickly weeds growing up through the floor of an abandoned shack full of sharp-fanged predators. Sophomores weren't The Evil of the place, but their mere existence added to the ambience. That they could be corporals and have authority over us seemed simply unusual and cruel.

One particular gargoyle who was to be elevated that spring was skinny, with freckles and sort of bulging eyes. He also had a high-pitched, squeaky voice which grated like fingernails on a blackboard. In a world of mouth-breathing menaces, this nineteen-year-old was an annoying blemish on an adolescent face.   Also, his name could have been that of a minor villain from the fertile pen of Charles Dickens.

A fair number of my classmates were gone by the spring, casualties either directly or indirectly of the plebe system. Those of us whose names were still on the M Company roster attributed our success to dysfunctional coping skills and the roll of the dice. The Presbyterians said it was the will of God. Regardless, the news of sophomore Corporals was shrugged by the knobs in the spirit of "It's always SOME thing." Our lives were miserable – sophomores with rank couldn't do anything new or more that would make any difference.

Not surprisingly, the sophomore who would be ranked first was the company clerk. Less digestible was the news that he of the freckles and squeaks was also among the few chosen to be high and lifted up. When I heard that, unlikely but plausibly, the annoying one was a corporal, I was surprised that my first reaction was an odd one of joy. I only determined the source of joy in reflection: *No kidding – he's a corporal?*

9. – BARRACKS ADMINISTRATION

9.14. GALLERIES AND STAIRWAYS

d. Running on the galleries and stairways is prohibited.

I first encountered my new chief as a leader of men when he was locked and loaded. With a few of his freshly promoted buddies, he was waiting for ducks like me in the blind at the stairwell. Among the usual waddling of freshmen, I tooled into the company area after the noon meal, racing along the outside 12-inches of pathway on the edge of the shooting gallery at 120 steps a minute. (NOTE: With a nod to *The Blue Book*, 120 steps a minute was a way of describing a brisk walk because running on the galleries was forbidden.) Ahead were the spiral stairs in the barracks corner and the ever-present risk of an encounter with some glorified goon.

"Halt, knobs!" the sophomore corporal squeaked.

We did, taking care that the glassy finish on our shoes did not come in contact with the heels immediately ahead. No doubt pleased that his very first command had worked, he then proceeded to vent his long-suppressed opinion of us as a group before running us on the stairs. Running on the stairs was a time-consuming ritual of up and down and up and down the four levels. It was an exercise which had become as entertaining to us as the sixth time around the little track with a three-year-old on a miniature railroad carnival ride. In the moment, all that mattered was squaring the trash cans at the gallery corners without touching them, not slipping on well-worn cement, and preserving the shine on the toes of our shoes.

"Halt!" cheeped again.

I was on my way up, a step below a memorable classmate who was poised on his way down. He was a sumo on the varsity wrestling team. The sophomore corporal threaded his way among us up the stairs with the purpose of confronting this particular grappler. The corporal stopped beside me. He looked up at my massive friend and began to point out his character flaws with the usual colorful adjectives peculiar to the barracks.

16. – CONDUCT

16.04. GENERAL RULES GOVERNING CONDUCT:

d. Censure: Deliberations or discussions among cadets or the outward expression having the object of conveying praise or censure towards their superiors or others in the service of the college are prohibited.

When my chief concluded his unfavorable appraisal, my eyes were supposed to be straight ahead and maybe they were – but I saw what I saw. My big friend raised his eyebrows and glanced down (WAY down) at his superior. Then from the back of his throat came the unmistakable snorting and slopping sound of a gathering ball of phlegm. I heard that sound in my subsequent life when I unwisely approached a llama in the Andes. The meaning that day was the same then, and the sound had the same result: I stepped away in the Andes. The corporal did likewise in the stairwell.

To my knowledge, nothing was ever said of this outward expression prohibited by *The Blue Book*. But it taught me to appreciate sophomores who were modestly endowed. I trained myself to keep them in mind when my knees felt wobbly while awaiting some pending academic report: I would find someone in the class ahead of me who I would have predicted could not possibly be in the class ahead of me and think, *"If he can do it, I can do it."*

Scientifically, this was a Darwinian conclusion which for me seemed merely a humble conceit. Also, my conscience was clear theologically because it is my firm belief that some of us are naturally elected to inspire others by serving as missing links.

By logic, becoming a sophomore myself was inevitable; by April, it was too late to turn back. Years earlier, I had learned how to click off those last few weeks of classroom meetings, day by day and even minute by minute. It was beach weather in Charleston, hope for summertime and freedom was rising, and the pathetic remnant of the plebe system was no more than a hollow echo in an empty trash can. I was a veteran, a survivor forged forever with my classmates into something new. Perhaps we were not prettier, but we were tougher. We were also strangely optimistic, even though it meant we would be sophomores.

YOU THINK I'M BAD, SIR? YOU OUGHT TO SEE KOWSNOFSKI.

(The) Shako,
Homecoming, 1964

Academic Year 1963-1964

I had a rich exposure to Bible teaching in my years before college. My father was an Episcopalian, my mother was a Baptist, and I had experience in the practices of both faiths. I also had experiences in Christian services conducted by ministers of other denominations in navy chapels. God and the Bible were part of public school routines in those days - even in the U.S. Navy dependent school I attended in the Philippines. My teachers often integrated scriptural wisdom with history, literature and science; music teachers especially seemed to prefer uplifting, classic sacred songs and spirituals.

11. – CHAPEL AND RELIGIOUS SERVICES

11.01. RULES FOR RELIGIOUS SERVICES:

a. All cadets will attend some form of religious services. Unless specifically excused they will attend Chapel on Sundays with the Corps.

At The Citadel in the '60s, chapel attendance was required. Each cadet was expected to declare and practice his preference for Sunday morning services. I began attending Protestant services in September of 1962. But in the second semester, my decision about Sunday services was determined more by pragmatism than theology. Sunday morning *Reveille* sounded an hour later than weekdays, so I decided to attend Episcopalian services, primarily because they were early – before breakfast.

The Episcopal Chapel formation was usually in the dark and relatively without drama for freshmen. The Episcopalian upperclassmen who supervised the formation were usually either too devout or too sleepy to bother us. We would return to breakfast, then bed, as the Protestants formed up out on the quad. Led by the Sunday color guard, they all marched formally across the parade ground as the Regimental Band played *Onward Christian Soldiers.*

In that first year of college, I was aware of others around me who were Jewish, Catholic and Orthodox Christian. I knew about this private part of their lives because of their chapel preferences. This led me to assume that we all took the teachings of our scriptural understanding to heart and accepted the standards which all of our faiths promoted. This had been my pre-collegiate assumption with my (in retrospect) remarkably benign high school friends. The first moral precept in *The Blue Book of 1960* seemed to reinforce this perspective:

The Citadel Code "earnestly commended to all cadets": To revere God, love my country, and be loyal to The Citadel. – Mark W. Clark, President

Without examining the obvious, I concluded that swearing and pornography in the barracks and consuming alcohol on general leave were legitimate signs of adult (Christian!) maturity and, as the General would say, becoming a "whole man." With this uninspected and naïve assumption in my teenage mind, I rationalized the raw reality of private cadet life as an adult extension of the Bible teachings of my childhood. In reflection, I believe this was the beginning of my developing a skill in compartmentalizing conflicting thoughts of theology, philosophy, psychology and science.

The mental capacity to keep truths separated would, one day, help me to pass qualifying exams for a medical career. Compartmentalizing also helped maintain my sanity as I stoically separated medical gore and human folly from the suffering individuals who would be my patients.

I did not process the foolishness of the thought that private debauchery was somehow inevitable, even sacred, until enough time had passed. Senseless experiences and emotionally charged moments in those days were simply uninspected and packed away somewhere. The natural emotions that I had suppressed as a freshman continued to bubble in my first months as a sophomore. Many years later I recovered a capacity to experience compassion. Now, I can write about this.

> **The Citadel Code** "earnestly commended to all cadets": To make friends with refined, cultivated and intellectual people. – Mark W. Clark, President

The friendships that I formed during the stress of my freshman year have been particularly enduring. The barracks was my home that year but not a safe place for a knob to relax and enjoy a friend's conversation.

On the quad and galleries, freshmen were either frozen or blurs. They were silent unless required to speak. Relaxed socializing for knobs occured off campus during weekend general leave. Otherwise moments might occur during a shared extra-curricular activity, on the athletic fields, or in free periods between classes at Mark Clark Hall. In my search for "refined, cultivated and intellectual people," I was finding only people like me.

Mom, I'm home.

(The) Shako, Spring, 1964

During my plebe year, I had been a zero among zeros. Friendships were unencumbered by differences in status. Then, after almost nine months as a plebe, I learned that when I returned from summer furlough I would be distinguished from others as a corporal. This news in May was unexpected, heartening and conflicting.

Ranking was partly determined by a numbered listing of each cadet in the company by class, as evaluated by others in the company. The balance rested with the Company Tactical Officer (tac), an advisor with whom I never had a memorable conversation. I had no idea what my ranking was in April of 1963 and didn't care until ranking news broke. My first reaction was that I had been honored by those who knew me. Immediately, my next thought was that I held sophomore corporals in low regard and I was about to become one of them.

15. – COMPANY ADMINISTRATION

15.01. DUTIES OF LEADERS:

h. The Corporal: The corporal is the assistant squad leader. He performs the duties of the squad leader when the latter is absent.

Rank was a challenge to character and ethics as well as an additional source of discord among friends who were already under pressure. So my second fall semester began with hope and uncertainty. I found that some of my friends who had been zeros like me, had hardened goals to distinguish themselves in the next years by "bucking" for more rank. Bucking for rank came with a cost which included time for "racking" knobs and reporting others, including classmates, who failed to keep *Blue Book* standards. It was part of the culture and expected of cadets with rank.

With the other corporals, I participated in harassing knobs on the galleries. But some of my classmates behaved more like the corporals of the previous year and I became conflicted about my own limited authority with freshmen. Being hard-bitten with knobs was more of an unpleasant expectation than an honor. Besides, knobs smelled bad. The question haunted me: *What must I look like to these unfortunate human beings?*

15. – COMPANY ADMINISTRATION

15.01. DUTIES OF LEADERS:

j. The Cadet Private: The Cadet Private except within scope of his authority when detailed on some duty expressly involving supervision of other cadets, has no authority to give orders to any other cadet.

Along with corporals, my circle of sophomore friends included certain privates who had deliberately set courses that trended away from the ideals of The Citadel Code. One of these deliberately determined to duck as many formations and classes as he could. Another's mind was set to accumulate exactly the number of academic credits required to graduate. (As a senior, he found that he received a "B" in a course which he calculated required a "C" to meet his goal. He had a private interview with his professor. The professor agreed to reduce the grade to a "C" and my friend, with some satisfaction, told me of his academic achievement as we assembled for our graduation ceremony.)

Eventually I realized that probably each cadet was drawing his own conclusion about truth and the incongruences of barracks life as measured by the unforgiving surveillance of *The Blue Book.* We weren't all the same. We each had our own goals, standards and values and these were becoming apparent as we walked around with our chins out.

Cadet privates have their own honored stories at The Citadel. Perhaps they were marginalized by the Commandant, but they received their rings and diplomas along with everyone else. It was not unusual to hear of them finding remarkable success after graduation. My older brother graduated as a cadet private and years later he retired as a distinguished, ranking naval officer.

The lifestyle of a cadet private had been modeled to my roommate and me when we were knobs by certain upperclassmen. We had come to know these worthies with no ambition for rank on almost familiar terms. We knew of the possibilities of skipping formations and that the upright, spit-and-polish existence we had practiced so well as knobs could be dramatically ducked with the luck of an upper class private.

HOW MANY DEMERITS DO YOU GET FOR VAGRANCY?

The Author, previously unpublished.

As knobs, we had often been reminded that we (or our parents) were paying for the intense interest of the upperclassmen who supervised us. "There's a place for you at Clemson," they used to say. We realized that the slackest seniors we knew did not have anything close to the freedom of a Clemson freshman – still, someday being a senior private seemed like a rewarding, if short-term goal.

The simple pleasures of "our" senior privates in the barracks had made an impression on my roommate. He returned to campus that fall as an unapologetic private without aspirations for rank. I knew him as an uncomplicated and really nice son of the Carolina upcountry. He was often way over his head in academics, but he had proven to be a very street-smart knob.

Since I wasn't in the competition for rank, I vicariously released my spirit to join my roommate and the many others who found an unassuming pride as cadet privates. My friends were my classmates and the year we were sophomores, it seemed beyond most of us to be refined, cultivated and intellectual. That year, incidentally, was the year of the Great Food Fight when the spirit of the Senior Private seemed to invest an entire battalion.

19. - DINING HALL

19.07. GENERAL RULES IN DINING HALL:

f. Gentlemanly manners and good conduct at the table will be required at all times. The throwing of food or missiles, tossing of any articles, shouting or unnecessarily loud talking, or any disorderly or improper conduct in the Dining Hall is prohibited.

At a noon meal, I was sitting in my company area of the 3rd Battalion section. From my seat, I had a full view of the open space beyond where the 1st Battalion was seated. For reasons I do not know, there was suddenly a marked silence in that area, followed immediately by cacophonous chaos. As though on command, the entirety of perhaps 450 cadets was yelling and heading for the tall grass, ducking, running and throwing food across the room. In that moment, the air was alive with bowls of mashed potatoes, pitchers of tea, salt shakers, dinner rolls, hilarity and high dudgeon. And that's all I know about the Great Food Fight beyond what I heard later: some heads rolled along with the buns. If a battalion of us looked like that, what chance did I have of finding any friends among the missing superior species commended by the General?

Eventually, the quality of my associations improved – at least off campus. Enriching my social life, another friendship outside of my Citadel circle began to provide a counterbalance to slipping along the slope with my minimalist friends. Over the summer, I found that I was in love. My girlfriend and I had dated since meeting in her church youth group during high school days. Her freshman year began at Furman University in Greenville, 200 miles away, when I returned to Charleston as a sophomore.

The first time we were together that fall was the occasion of spending fifty dollars of prize money I had won just before the conclusion of my plebe year. A fair-sized yacht had been donated to the college that spring and the President thought it needed cadet art work in the cabin. I submitted the oil painting that won the contest. That fall, in front of the artwork and along with the check, I stood with the General for a photograph in the cabin. At the first opportunity, my girl and I shared our very first porterhouse steak at one of the few elegant restaurants in Charleston, funded by that famous patron of the arts, Mark Clark.

I was fairly clueless about affairs of the heart, but I knew I had struck gold as our relationship ripened. I also sensed that sooner or later, my drift toward indolence would bring on a crisis in my love life. My girl was no slacker and had little tolerance for foolishness. She was a serious student and inspired me to apply myself to my studies. She certainly qualified as one of the "refined, cultivated and intellectual people" which the General "earnestly commended" I befriend. In fact, she was my best proof of a friend who met his expectations. Also, my private buddies liked her, too.

(The) Shako,
Spring, 1965

I didn't know it in my sophomore year, but today I realize that my brain was operating in a riptide of learning convergent and divergent thinking. I had done okay in high school chemistry, biology and physics. As a high school senior, I enjoyed a year-long course in creative writing which required the submission of an original short story, essay or poem each Friday. I also spent two semesters, two hours a day, sketching, drawing and painting under the direction of an accomplished art teacher. I had learned much and he had encouraged me to follow an art pathway after graduation. So I considered myself a budding artist when I was applying for college admissions.

Artists are numbered among those creative individuals who connect dots of information in ways that look more like the complex traces of a spider web than a straight, interstate highway across Nevada. True artists think "outside the box" and find multiple, possible solutions before the single best answer. Their brains are wired differently from others and in their hearts, artists are divergent thinkers.

I WAS JUST SITTING HERE THINKING ABOUT ... OH, YOU KNOW ... THINGS..

(The) Shako, Graduation, 1964

I had been accepted in art at two respected institutions and was considering which to prefer when my father commented, "A Bachelor of Science will be more useful; you can learn art later." This led to an application and acceptance at The Citadel. My father then said, "In art school, you will be one of a school full of artists. At The Citadel, you could be the artist of the college." This settled my decision because it was my policy to listen to my father. I admired him and besides, he was paying for it.

The Citadel Code "earnestly commended to all cadets": To be diligent in my academic studies and my military training. – Mark W. Clark, President

From early in my career as a student, my parents expected honest results. But they never seemed to be concerned how I made the sausage of good grades. So on my own hook and long before I was a cadet, I had developed habits of procrastination with academic preparations until the deadline was looming. Then I would sprint to the finish by last minute cramming.

I knew my only path to a B.S. degree at The Citadel would be in Pre-Medicine, even though I had no ambition to be a physician. The elementary math courses I had passed taught me convergent thinking for solutions in mathematics. The science majors required a divergent competency in advanced math beyond my abilities. College-level chemical math required thinking that produced mostly headaches and few correct solutions. I knew how to sink Number 2 barracks because that's how my mind worked. Though I was unaware of my mind's operations then, I knew that chemical math could sink me.

Receiving Classroom Instruction

How learning actually occurs is a fascination of science. As a student of science, I became very familiar with teachers in classrooms and on one occasion, I made my own humble effort to advance the study of how learning occurs. In a particular class, the instructor read from notes and habitually seemed to be addressing the far corner of the room, apparently oblivious to the languid learning habits of the individuals in the class. So, I documented their methods of learning for my own study. I don't remember what he was teaching – but as you can see, I was busy learning. The Author, previously unpublished.

Knowing nothing about convergence and divergence, I began the chemistry course of "Qualitative Analysis." At The Citadel, this was the single, critical course that had a reputation for diverting pre-med students into business administration. By the end of the semester, I had one dominant, convergent thought: I was in the wrong major. The high wall of scientific academics that I faced convinced me to give up on gold stars. Passing became the only relevant standard.

It seemed that the only learning I accomplished in Qual was efficient ducking. There was a moment when I was deep in thought (or deep in confusion – I can't remember.) The professor, a member of the Greatest Generation, apparently misinterpreted my posture and facial expression as evidence that I was disconnected, if not asleep. I saw him in a moment rear back with his piece of chalk and rifle it at my head. I tipped my head slightly to the left as the missile that was converging toward my ear zipped past. My evasion satisfied him that I was still with him, so without comment, he resumed his lecture.

(The) Shako, Spring, 1965

Classroom speed bumps were routine that fall as my artist brain reeled with alien issues of science. But I am more embarrassed to recall that semester as a sophomore corporal in the barracks. I had survived my first year sequestered like a heretic monk, silenced in a Spanish monastery during the Inquisition. It was such a contrast to simply walk through the sally port without worrying about taking a head shot that I relaxed more than was wise. Now I realize I was just a teenager with more hormones than sense, adjusting to a menacing environment which had become familiar and where some of the worse threats had been attenuated. This is probably why sophomores proved themselves to be knobs with their chins out.

My roommate was a science major, so he and I were often in the same classrooms and labs. Our bookshelves featured onerous science textbooks with more information than we would ever know, nagging us to pay them some attention. But in off-hours, we preferred conversation, playing touch football – anything but studying.

Before November, I was still a corporal but I had dropped my own standards to the alternate path of privates who commanded no authority. By my roomie's unintentional influence and without fully noticing, I had set my own course by his star. The earliest symptoms of the dissolute track we had chosen became evident in our room during "evening study period." *The Blue Book of 1960* had admonishments in abundance concerning barracks conduct during ESP:

9. – BARRACKS ADMINISTRATION

9.06. CALL TO QUARTERS

(5) (b) All cadets will observe study hours from call to quarters after supper until taps from Sunday through Thursday inclusive except as follows:

(1) Cadets may retire after 2130 hours.

6. – ALL RIGHT AND ALL IN

6.01. MEANING OF REPORTS:

a. The report "all right" means:

(2) From any occupant of a room at any inspection: That all absentees and all visitors present are authorized.

b. The report "all in" means:

(1) From any occupant of a room at taps inspection or at the inspection ten minutes after the termination of general leave: That all persons present or absent are authorized.

9. – BARRACKS ADMINISTRATION

9.24. – VISITING:

e. Evening Study Periods: Visiting during Evening Study Period until tattoo *(sic)* is forbidden.

About an hour after returning from supper, the bugler played *Call to Quarters* and all cadets had to be either in their rooms or have a solid reason for being absent. The galleries at 1930 hours (7:30 p.m.) were alive with "division checkers" banging on door after door, calling out "All right?" From within each room came either "All right" or an explanation that had better be truthful.

ESP was a time of enforced study until the *Tattoo* bugle sounded at 2200 hours (10:00 p.m.) Traditionally this was supposed to be when lights were going out and peace was settling like a fog over the day's activities. In the barracks, it was a time to finish up on racking freshmen, banging on the packaged food machines for change, and one last run to the latrines. *Taps* then finished the day, along with a final division check at the closed door: BANG! "All in?" - "All in."

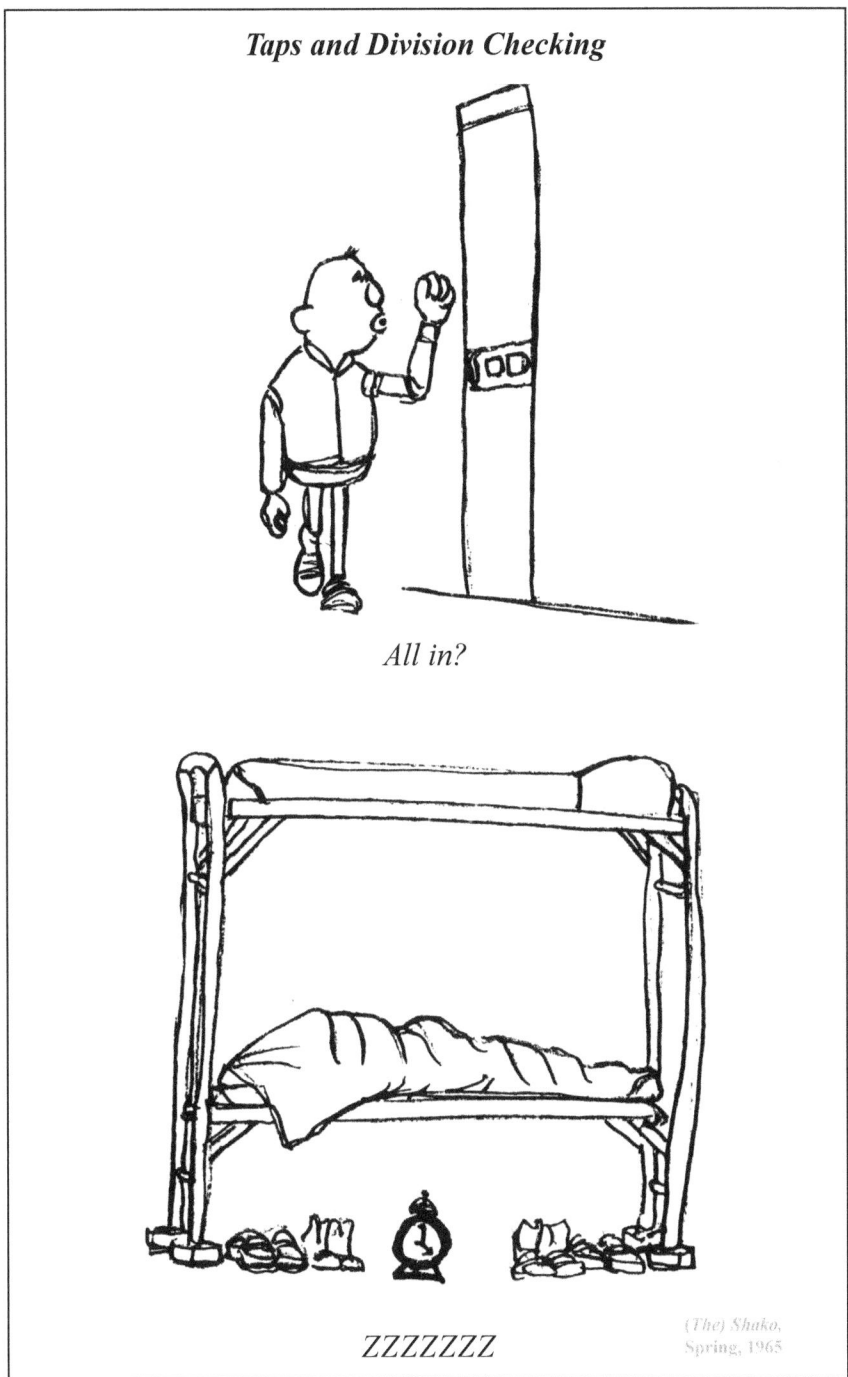

Taps and Division Checking

All in?

ZZZZZZZ

(The) Shako,
Spring, 1965

The Sphinx,
calendar, 1965

Often ESP was squandered in silly games and socializing. Sometimes when the pressure was on, we pulled "all-nighters" of study to make up for our poor use of time. These late hours of desperation had the bonus stress of being *Blue Book* violations:

9. – BARRACKS ADMINISTRATION

9.16. LIGHTS: a. Except on nights of General Leave, lights will be turned off at taps.

9.21. ROOMS:

d. Ventilation: Rooms will be kept well-ventilated at all times. Door transoms will be kept open.

In the '60s, rooms were kept well-ventilated because they were without air-conditioning. As *Taps* was haunting the quadrangle on all-nighters, we would rig a blanket at the transom and close it, blocking the light from inside. At the same time, we would cover our window to the outside with another blanket so that light through the window would not reveal our nocturnal dysfunction.

Closing the transom and window meant turning the room into an oven. Years later, wisdom would speak that this risk with regulations was best avoided by developing better study habits. But I was a sophomore and that social class is not known for wisdom.

9. – BARRACKS ADMINISTRATION

9.21. ROOMS:

c. Cleanliness of Rooms: The rooms will be kept free from dust and dirt. All ledges, shelves, and washboards will be kept clean. Brasses will be polished, leather goods shined, and books and papers will be neatly arranged.

25. – INSPECTION

25.07. IRREGULAR INSPECTION: Barracks may be inspected at any hour of the day or night by the Officer in Charge, the Commandant, Tactical Officers, or the Officer of the Day or Guard.

About this time, my slide toward dereliction was exposed by anonymous authority figures on an unscheduled room inspection one morning. I learned of my deficiencies when I returned from classes for dinner formation: everything – everything – in my room had been stacked on the gallery outside my door. *The Blue Book* enforcers had prevailed over my sophomoric condition. My roommate and I spent the afternoon reassembling our room by the book.

18. – DEMERITS

18.01. WHEN AWARDED: All justified delinquency reports entered against a cadet shall be cause for the imposition of one or more demerits depending on the degree of delinquency. Demerits are not considered punishment but a system of rating cadets in conduct.

A few days later, my sins were posted on the company bulletin board to inform those who had missed the drama. I would face two weeks of restrictions and confinements. I was also "awarded" five demerits.

37. – PUNISHMENT

37.01. – IMPOSITION OF PUNISHMENT

c. Demerits and punishment for offenses of the Second Class shall be imposed by the Commandant of Cadets with the approval of the President.

37.03. DURATION OF TOURS: A punishment tour shall be fifty minutes duration with ten minutes between tours. Rifles will be carried by all cadets.

I walked some tours in the spring of my freshman year. Fifty minutes back and forth with a rifle on the quadrangle of Number 2 barracks during free time was truly a nuisance. Similar to a tour - in frustration, if not in discomfort - a confinement was two hours in uniform at my desk. But tours and confinements were not considered a disgrace by most of my friends – they were part of the culture. From their time spent walking tours and enduring confinements, many of my friends learned to be smarter in skirting the rules. For me, tours and confinements brought sobering reminders that I could do better. Alone in my room, I had some glimpses of purpose and the future. Did I want to spend the next years accepting the rules and practicing self-discipline or resisting the rules and taking my chances? Was I a hypocrite to accept corporal stripes as I carelessly acted like a fatuous dolt?

The *Sphinx* calendar, 12/120 cover, 1965

These thoughts flowed in the context of larger questions. Did I want to better myself? If not, why was I a cadet when I could be a carefree sophomore at some other college in some other major? There were no magic moments at that time. But without insight, I now see that my path into adulthood was laid out by decisions I would make in the second semester of my sophomore year.

When I returned from furlough for the spring semester, things had changed. My Qualitative Analysis grade was posted on the door of the classroom in Bond Hall. I had passed Qual with a "D - - -" (that is, a D-minus-minus-minus.) It wasn't pretty or something to write home about. But that D- - - was the most difficult, critical and valuable grade I ever received as a student. Passing Qual determined for me that I would stick with my pre-med major.

In the classes required for my major were cadets who were deliberately preparing for medical school. As a group, these distinguished themselves from the rest of us by being more focused on grades. They also seemed to be more competitive in lab results and concerned about question-answer comparisons after exams. Sometimes they seemed relieved when others received bad news about grades. Also, if they knew I had done well, my future doctor friends seemed glad when I reassured them that I had no medical school aspirations. I tried to avoid these post-mortem conversations.

No professor sat down with me and discussed my future plans. Specifically, none of the professors in my major spoke with me about a future in medicine. Privately, I felt some stress in my major classes and labs because I had fallen so far after earning gold stars as a freshman. But no professor or classmate asked about that either. My parents knew of my grades and were relieved at the news of my passing Qual simply because I was so relieved. Otherwise, no comments.

This springtime of cerebral tossed salad came with a shadowy dressing on the side - I wasn't sure that my girlfriend at Furman intended to stay on the path with me. Communication was a physical problem for us because of the two hundred miles between us. Access to the phone was limited and pay phones were expensive (10-cents), inconvenient and too public. So our contact was primarily through frequent letters. I looked forward to her letters, especially because there was something on them that smelled good. (If mine smelled like where I lived, I appreciate her even more.)

As the weather was warming up in Charleston, I started noticing that she was casually mentioning some guy named Fred in her life upstate. It was "Fred and I" doing this and that. After a few weeks, her letters compelled me to do something, too. I was probably also influenced by the *Tams* in the background music of the mess hall asking me what kind of fool she thought I was.

16. – CONDUCT

16.04. GENERAL RULES GOVERNING CONDUCT:

j. Doing the Right Thing: Whenever circumstances over which he has no control make it necessary for a cadet to violate orders or regulations in order to do the obviously right thing the cadet will report the fact to the Commandant as soon as possible.

At the time, I was unaware that *The Blue Book* played a role in the conduct of my love life. (This lack of awareness, of course, would not be accepted as an excuse.) Also, I don't remember thinking that the Commandant would even care about this personal matter. But I knew the right thing to do. After Saturday Morning Inspection, I walked through the main gate in my dress uniform with some pocket change and began hitch-hiking to Greenville for a conference with my girl concerning Fred.

The Citadel Code "earnestly commended to all cadets": To take pride in my uniform and in the noble traditions of the college and never do anything that would bring discredit upon them. – Mark W. Clark, President

I was aware that many South Carolinians seemed to feel sorry for cadets, so I was confident that someone would fall for a pitiable pilgrim in uniform. I set out just before noon for the interstate which was completed to about ten miles away, the western edge of Charleston County. I knew I looked good in my "salt and pepper" and proceeded in the assurance that I was doing the right thing, operating in the noble traditions, etc. I'll bet the President would have done the same thing.

> **27.02. GENERAL LEAVE:** Defined: General leave is permission for all eligible members of the Corps of Cadets to be absent from The Citadel Campus for a definite period. Cadets who are on general leave may visit places within twenty-five (25) miles of The Citadel.

After more than an hour, I had not found the combination of compassionate drivers who would help me reach the interstate. So I visited a sequence of places within the twenty-five mile rule until almost midafternoon. I reached the Furman campus before supper and found my girl in the library. (This was the first place to look for her on a Saturday, being one of those "refined, cultivated, and intellectual people" who the General "earnestly commended" to me as an associate.)

She was mildly surprised to see me and seemed bemused at the reason for my advent. In the cafeteria over a hamburger, I spoke briefly and earnestly about my commitment to her and asked that she figure out how Fred fit into our relationship and let me know. (Secretly, I was hoping that my uniform would seal the deal over a civilian college Joe. Or Fred.)

30. – OFFENSES

30.01. OFFENSES CLASSIFIED:

c. Offenses of the First Class:

(6) Going beyond cadet limits without leave.

23. – HITCH-HIKING

23.01. Hitch-hiking or asking for rides by cadets in uniform is forbidden.

I traveled back by the same cut-and-paste transportation method. Knowing that I had done the right thing, I slept well that night. I was blissfully unaware of my *Blue Book* frowning silently from its hook on my door, so I did not inform the Commandant that I had done the right thing. Ultimately, my adventure was a success. Those who could have brought me to grief remained unaware and Fred stopped prowling around the trash cans near the window of my girl's dorm room.

(The) Shako,
Spring, 1965

16. – CONDUCT

16.04. GENERAL RULES GOVERNING CONDUCT:

bb.   Unnecessary Noises: Cadets will not create unnecessary noise in quadrangles, barracks, dining hall, or other college buildings.   Yelling, calling to other cadets in a loud tone, loud whistling, loud playing of radios or record players, or slamming of doors are forbidden.

The nadir of my debauchery as a sophomore was eventually arrested by the battalion commander. The day before his intervention therapy, I had been inadvertently caught up in some kind of small riot begun by others on the way back from mess. When the brawl reached the barracks, the miscreants were shouting and throwing things. Something flew by me and I threw it back. I probably shouted as well. I really don't remember.

But the next day we were in full dress on the quadrangle prepared for retreat parade. The battalion commander in all his finery walked deliberately over to me. From a few inches away, he spoke evenly of my participation in the disorder of the day before. For a moment, I fought the words which were stuttering around inside my head like a ticker tape: *But there were others. I didn't start it. I wasn't nearly as bad as the rest.*

28. - MILITARY COURTESY

28.05. COURTESIES AMONG CADETS:

b. Cadets shall make use of the word "Sir" in answering official questions asked by cadet commissioned officers or cadets acting as such.

Sophomores usually did not address upperclassmen as "Sir." But this situation, in this formal setting with this particular conversation, was different. I replied, also evenly: "Yes, sir. No excuse, sir."

Meanwhile, on a hopeful note, I had opened a window and found a breath of fresh air when I committed to being an artist with *The Shako*. Cartoon characters I had drawn for high school yearbooks had been influenced by the artists of *Mad Magazine*. The sardonic quality of my humor had been inherited from my father and sharpened by the pen of James Thurber in *The New Yorker*. As a sophomore, I was experimenting with the cartoons I was submitting for publication, searching for my style.

My contributions to *The Shako* apparently stimulated the editors of *The Sphinx,* the college yearbook, to make a contact. In February, I was privately visiting with some of the most prominent seniors during ESP (with authorization) and sketching their portraits. They had been chosen by their classmates as "senior superlatives" and their images in

The 1964 Sphinx are my pencil art. Two months later, I illustrated the cover of a "folio" published for the English Department's celebration of Shakespeare's 400th birthday observance.

Becoming a Combat Artist

"Awright, awright—it's a general!
Ya wanna pass in review?"

Cartoon by Bill Mauldin in *Up Front*,
pg. 17, copyright 1945; author's library.

*Years later, I now realize that my main inspiration for **The Shako** cartoons came from Bill Mauldin, the creator of "Willie and Joe." Bill Mauldin and I were about the same age when we left our respective homes, me to The Citadel, Mauldin eventually to Italy in World War II. His humor was based on the reality of two G.I.s in the European war. Willie and Joe were a hit with the troops in **Stars and Stripes**, the official U.S. military newspaper. I grew up around Willie and Joe as a child, enjoying hours with them in Mauldin's book, **Up Front**.*

Bill Mauldin's commander was the same General who would become my college president. Mark Clark had defended Mauldin and his work as good for the morale of the troops when General George Patton took official offense at the debauched state of Willie and Joe.

Today, it occurs to me that maybe General Clark made it possible for me to continue in my work at The Citadel. Maybe it was the spirit of Willie and Joe in my cartoons that he recognized and permitted.

(The) Shako, Spring, 1963

In 1962, 44 freshman cadet recruits were on the M Company roster. A year later, 22 sophomores reported for the fall term. By the end of my sophomore year, the class of '66 roster in the company had been pruned further. Much of the attrition was due to academic deficiencies from that first year which were too great to repair. The losses and continuing academic problems of a number of my classmates led to disqualifications and a skewing in the ranking for the year. I was ranked artificially higher as a result and anticipated promotion to staff sergeant as a junior. I had matured in my understanding of the meaning of the rank by then. I wanted the higher rank because I was ready to learn about using authority effectively.

WHERE DID MY BRAIN GO?
I KNOW IT'S AROUND HERE
SOMEWHERE.

(The) Shako,
Graduation, 1964
The Author
and
Kevin Metzger

I had learned that I wasn't much of a scientist, but I was thinking more like a scientist than I had in high school. Also, my father was right: I was on a path to becoming the school artist. I had found my niche among a variety of friends and also my place in the chain-of-command as a subordinate.

With more freedom in the barracks and around campus, I learned more about classmates in other battalions. In scattered, unplanned conversations, I often heard stories that were amusing and variably alarming. While we were all experiencing similar circumstances and stresses, we were responding differently. I still had no interest in bucking for rank. But neither did I have the cavalier spirit necessary to enjoy being a senior private someday. I was okay with submitting to authority, going along with expectations, and paying the price for failure when necessary. Meanwhile, my friendships had become valuable to me and I sensed that the day might come when asserting authority could spoil a relationship.

Without the straitjacket of the plebe system, I was enjoying downtime again. In Mark Clark Hall or on general leave, I made friends with some who regularly left campus (authorized or otherwise) for tippling at convenient taverns such as the Ark or Big John's. I had friends who had pets in their rooms and a few who were partners in beach cottage leases. Some were hunting quail, sailing and sky-diving; one guy was a regular player in an on-going Charleston bridge tournament. Oh - and I heard of friends who were married.

But my best and most significant friend was in a college 200 miles away. She was unintentionally pushing me to the higher standard required by my conscience – the one that was closer to my ideals. I really did want to live by the Cadet Code. I agreed with my girl and the General about the code but wasn't making my best effort to reach the higher standard. Obviously, I had a problem with integrity.

Passing Qualitative Analysis had settled the issue of my academic major. I knew I would be going for a Bachelor of Science in Pre-medicine. But the D minus-minus-minus and my disturbing insight into my character flaws and the limitations of my brain, were evidence that there probably were no future stars for me as a pre-med major. Oddly, though, there was hope in this part of my life.

My brain was changing in the way it was working. Even though my artistic muse was still messing around in my head, there was a scientist tinkering around in there, too. The hours spent in laboratories were causing me to think more logically. I was also categorizing facts better, storing them more efficiently, and retrieving them quicker. Scientific analysis and thinking logically would be important in accurate diagnosis and midnight decisions in the future.

My actual thoughts about the future, however, were still ambivalent. They included the thought that there may be no future. These were the times of Soviet expansion, intercontinental ballistic missiles, and the draft. I was registered with selective service when the Cuban missile crisis occurred in October of 1962. My hepatitis had me upside down as I listened to every bomber in America roar above, on the way to Florida. My brother, standing somberly at my infirmary bed that evening, told me that if anything happened, I should get home and take care of our grandparents. He would try to find us later.

Nothing happened. But in the spring of 1964, I spent an afternoon in a King Street theater watching Dr. Strangelove rise up from his invalid's chair rejoicing as Major King Kong yippee-ki-yayed past his bomb bay doors. I walked out in the bright sunlight, wondered how a movie about nuclear annihilation had made me laugh, bought another admission ticket, and watched it all again.

Meanwhile, back in the barracks, the General distributed to each of us a paperback to read along with *The Blue Book*. It was a best-seller in 1964 that warned of communist fellow-travelers in the American government. All of this to explain my ambivalence about a future which could include going "toe-to-toe with the Rooskies," as Major Kong had hoped. When I was a sophomore, I only knew that if I was still standing after graduation, I would be in a U.S. military uniform. I just couldn't think past that.

The Citadel Code "earnestly commended to all cadets": To improve my mind by reading and participation in intellectual and cultural activities. – Mark W. Clark, President

(The) Shako.
Spring, 1964

My cultural life began to improve when I was asked to assist artistically in the English Department's celebration of the 400th anniversary of Shakespeare's birth. I also won some prize money in a sonnet competition for this event.

Then I was invited to join the Round Table and connect with some of those cultivated people commended by the General. The Round Table was an honor society of upperclassmen and a few of the faculty and staff. I became the rising art editor for *The Shako* and began practicing with the Sunday color guard which was forming for the fall semester. I was no longer sailing for the unpretentious port of a senior private. I was becoming busy.

My renewed interest in finding a more excellent way (as the Apostle might say) was primarily inspired by my girl in Greenville. We had no spoken agreement, but intuitively I knew that I was her guy. I also knew that I was a disappointment. She was too much of a lady to speak of my shortcomings but I knew she knew them and that my standards were inadequate. It wasn't a conscious thought at the time.

> **The Citadel Code** "earnestly commended to all cadets": To perform every duty with fidelity and conscientiousness and to make DUTY my watchword. – Mark W. Clark, President

Today I believe that the General's code of conduct and the hopes of my girl that I would do my duty were critical. Of course, I was familiar with the concept of "duty." When I was eight years old I would promise to "do my duty" each month at Cub Scout meetings. A plaque in the barracks reminded me daily of a quotation (perhaps) from Robert E. Lee: "Duty is the sublimest word in the English language."

My main source of extra income as a high schooler came from babysitting in the neighborhood. I practiced being faithful with obligations as I watched over and worked with children. I had also kept obligations to meet deadlines in high school as art editor for my senior yearbook. The two years at The Citadel had convinced me that it was my duty to comply with commands. But as responsibilities began to multiply at the end of my second year, I was learning the importance of efficiency, accuracy and prioritizing in fulfilling duty.

I don't remember resolving to make "duty" my watchword in 1964. But when I signed up for optional extra-curricular commitments, I determined to complete them satisfactorily. Volunteering free moments to *The Sphinx* and *The Shako* were ways to require me to press on toward higher challenges of duty. The skills I was practicing my sophomore year would someday play into passing medical exams and dedicated service in emergency rooms.

Meanwhile, in Round Table meetings, I enjoyed rich exchanges with upperclassmen and faculty. These conversations expanded the boundaries of my understanding and introduced me to alternate ways of seeing things. Someday, these early contacts would give me the broader perspective necessary to work with patients from across society, some of whom would hold astounding viewpoints and prejudices.

> **The Citadel Code** "earnestly commended to all cadets": To resolve to carry its standards into my future and to place right above gain and a reputation for integrity above power. – Mark W. Clark, President

My sophomore year, the answers to exam questions concerning qualitative analysis may have eluded me. But I confirmed the most important question I needed to answer. It came from the book of regulations which had guided my life before *The Blue Book: "How can a young man keep his way pure?"* I also knew the right answer from that same book: *"By keeping it according to Your word."* (Psalm 119:9, New American Standard Bible, 2020). That was the year I committed to going the right way.

My friends were my classmates. The year we were sophomores, it seems most of us just couldn't be refined, cultivated and intellectual people. By the end of the second semester, that reality gradually improved. Many of us were changing for the better, even if we couldn't appreciate it at the time. For my part, this was actually intentional. I knew I could do better and wanted to change.

As an upperclassman, I considered my sophomore year to have been the loss of two semesters. Years later, I now realize that it was the year I stabilized important foundations for my future. That year, I had some brushes with higher authority which taught me I should stay on the right side of the law. I made decisions about my heart, my brain, and my values that ultimately led me into a lifelong marriage, successful fatherhood and a forty year career in medicine. My decisions also set the stage for a peaceful retirement and kept me out of jail.

Photograph from the author's collection.

The Award-winning Quartet at the Talent Show

Folk-singing groups were popular in 1964, from the Kingston Trio to Peter, Paul and Mary. In remembering that year as one of my most significant, I must include the cultural triumph of the quartet composed of my brother, his roommate and me. (We never could enlist the fourth troubadour.) We sang a Smothers Brothers ballad of "Green Stamps" and for an encore, a passionate rendition of "Pity the Poor Caterpillar." The moment in the photo is big brother rending "...pity the goo, that sticks to your shoe." We won a special trophy on condition that we never sing on campus again.

Above Illustrations *(The) Shako,* Spring, 1964

To honor this watershed year of my life, I reconnected with the muse who led me to write the winning sonnet of the Shakespeare Quadricentennial celebration. I am not particularly proud of my winning poem. Sixty years later, that winner looks – well, sophomoric. So I submit this next verse, with appropriate modesty, to demonstrate my experience with convergent and divergent thinking through the traditional constraints of a proper sonnet form – 14 lines of iambic pentameter, rhymed ab, ab, cd, cd, ef, ef, gg. This is in honor of the Bard:

Sonnet #2

A sonnet is a verse of ordered form,

Arranged in ranks of rhyme with patterned pace.

Attention to alignment is the norm,

As cadence and accordance hold their place.

A sonnet marches by in fine array:

Its uniforms and banners pass with pride;

Its purpose is its order on display.

(Its message finds a place within to hide.)

But Shakespeare buzzed along a different trail

That darted back and forth from bloom to comb.

He ordered it contained to no avail

As nectar begat honey in his poem.

His message, not his method was his sonnet.

When Shakespeare was commander, he was on it.

(The) Shako,
Homecoming, 1964

Academic Years 1964-1966

As a junior, I returned to campus a little early after summer furlough because I was part of the freshman training cadre. We had a few required days of orientation before the arrival of the new class.

I had been spuriously advanced in rank again, because, as in the year before, classmates ranked above me were academically deficient or else failed to return. My roommate, who had drifted in the academic doldrums for two years, also finally swamped and dropped out of school. Over half of those who had begun as freshmen in M Company in September of 1962 were simply gone.

I had heard that the attrition of my M Company classmates was unusual and that our experiences with hazing as freshmen were not prevelant in the Corps. But I also knew that cadets applied the word "tradition" to whatever was done the year before and whatever might be called "normal" in cadet experiences was beyond verifying year-to-year and company-to-company.

(The) Shako,
Homecoming, 1964

As my junior year began, there occurred larger changes in the college that were significant to cadet culture, presuming that is a valid oxymoron. The most important change was that we had two new Generals on campus, one to serve as dean, the other as Commandant of Cadets. The dean was a Citadel graduate who had been a friend of my uncle; in more recent years, he had been a chemistry professor. I had never spoken to him but had heard that he was a nice guy. The new Commandant, on the other hand, quickly achieved a reputation as a piece of work.

1. – THE CHARACTER OF THE COLLEGE

1.03. LEADERSHIP STANDARDS:

Cadets entering the college are placed on an equality of opportunity to be trained in leadership. Instruction will be supervised and thorough. The abuse of authority by one who has obtained seniority in class or by appointment is an evidence of failure and will not be tolerated.

The new Commandant had been a highly successful combat commander of paratroopers in WW2; his office was in the new military science building, Jenkins Hall. From the start, he proved to be an advocate of *The Blue Book* and an agent of change in the barracks. I first saw him in action on the quad during plebe week when he confronted a classmate in another company dealing with knobs. Without ceremony, he literally removed my friend's sergeant stripes pin from his collar in front of the squad of freshmen.

(The) Shako,
Spring, 1965

As reports of other confrontations with authority accumulated, it was clear that the plebe system that I had known was undergoing a radical adjustment, ordered from the top. The new Commandant soon made being busted for hazing fashionable among the upper classes. Those who persisted in challenging the standards of *The Blue Book* went deeper underground in their extra-curricular activities. Personally, I had been exhausted by the system as a freshman and usually had other things on my mind. I think most of the juniors who were on cadre in M Company were similarly predisposed.

As a ranking junior in the company, I was qualified to try for a position on the Junior Sword Drill. This elite squad of fourteen ranking juniors endured weeks of rigorous training to perform a complex, public drill without spoken command only once. But their performance each November at the Ring Hop was always memorable.

I briefly felt some shame when I turned down the invitation. Practically, I was fairly certain that I would not qualify, just as I wouldn't have qualified for a varsity sports team as a "walk-on." I enjoyed physical activities and the bond that forms among members of disciplined teams. But the rigors of the Junior Sword Drill were more than I wanted to face that fall. As a consolation, I decided to honor my classmates on the Sword Drill through my art.

So I went to some of the Sword Drill evening practices in the athletic field house.

I was struck by the precision of the cadets practicing their exaggerated, high stepping routine with their flashing swords. Even more, I was impressed by how well they controlled the physical power required for the drill. I focused my attention on an M Company friend, Tom, who was the highest ranked junior in the battalion. Tom had proven to be an effective leader in the company. I realized later that it was his humility, not the glory of the Sword Drill, that made me want to draw him. I sketched what I saw and took my drawings back to my room to produce a cover for the fall edition of *The Shako*, in time for the Ring Hop.

Sketches of Sword Drill Practices

Sword drill practices were difficult for me to witness because of the obvious physical stress my friends were experiencing. Sketching them was easier.

The Author, previously unpublished

Using a white, wax-based pencil on black paper, I produced a dramatic, high-contrast rendering. I knew that it might be problematic for the printer so I personally carried my art over to the campus print shop. That was when I met the printer named "Red" and made a new friend.

Red gave it his best shot but eventually told me that the stark white on black image was beyond his skills to reproduce as a cover. In those days before computerized graphic art, my choices were limited. I could redo the art in a different medium or clip the figure and paste it on a lighter background. I couldn't face redoing the drawing, so we compromised with the final cover. But in the disappointment, there was a bonus for me: during this time, the cadet I had drawn for the cover became my new roommate and ultimately, Tom was one of my life-long best friends.

A big event of that fall for many upperclassmen was a football game with Army at West Point. Qualified cadets with the funds were authorized to travel on a midnight train to New York, spending Saturday night in a hotel in New York City after the game. My father, a former West Point cadet, had recently signed with the U.S. Agency for International Development. He, with my mother and two teenage brothers, had entered orientation for a family move to Saigon as I returned to college in 1964. He was now earning extra money because of his new job and thought spending some on a train ticket and hotel room for me was a good idea. So I was treated to an overnight in NYC.

I had tapped around the perimeter of the administration's toleration for my *Shako* cartoons for two years. In the fall of 1964, I probed the minefield a little further with a cartoon-troubled article titled "*The Shako* Gets to the Point." In the rearview mirror, I now see that my published cartoons and articles of sixty years ago were my contribution to speaking out against tyranny. From my experiences in those days, I came to understand what Socrates was thinking with his dying words after the authorities of Athens gave him the hemlock: "*Don't forget to sacrifice a rooster to Asclepius.*"

Excerpts from *The Shako*, vol. 33, fall 1964, no.1 (with commentary) follow:

> "*Our Friday classes seemed longer than usual as we waited for three o'clock and the little man on the microphone to say "Attention to orders: This is First Call for the West Point trip." But three o'clock did come, as I suspected it would all along, and we soon debarked (sic) by bus to the train station, after a slight pause. It seems that one of the tac officers boarded the "King Street-Citadel" bus instead, rode the bus one complete journey, and got off at Lesesne Gate, thinking to himself (I suppose) what a short trip it was to West Point and how rapid today's modern transportation is.*"

The story of the train trip included details of the boxed lunches we received and handed around:

> "*We had no trouble serving lunch ourselves – we had been doing it since Cadre because the Freshmen cannot be disturbed whilst they eat. (Fourth Class manual, Part IV, par. C., for those of you who should have but didn't.)*"

General Clark released some pigeons at half-time. I no longer remember why. If they were carrying a message, it might have read, "Being overrun – request air strike." The NYC newspaper reported that the real cadets had a "scrimmage" with The Citadel and would play their opening game the following weekend with an actual institution of higher learning.

So we traveled home Sunday, reaching campus just in time for Monday classes and the end of the story: *"I don't know how the rest of you all did Monday morning but those of us who had Military first period fared pretty well – you can't beat fifty minutes sleeping to really pep you up – if you know what I mean."*

This set of images is a rearrangement of the original Shako article.

HOMECOMING ISSUE, 1964   9

(The) Shako, Homecoming, 1964

There was no brass push-back concerning this submission for publication. From this, I learned that I had not yet crossed the line for acceptable commentary. Since childhood, I fundamentally accepted proper authority. But at The Citadel, I learned to successfully object to hubris in the expression of authority. I was content with this start, knowing that in me there was more – so much more.

My encouragement was still fresh when editors of *The 1965 Sphinx* asked me to produce a cartoon-illustrated calendar to raise money for the yearbook. It would be sold in time for Christmas shopping to customers who lived behind locked gates and were famous for being broke. The editors wanted me to tell it like it was in the year 1965. So began my artistic journey that would illustrate life in the Old Corps.

Most of my original published drawings are long gone, like the old Citadel print shop. But I retained some, and among them is the collection that comprised *The Sphinx* calendar of 1965. They are in the original India ink which pooled in the little rubber-stoppered bottle I used to dip my artist's pen into. I drew them in the fall of 1964, but I was thinking of next year - November of 1965 - when I would be a senior, kissing my girl in glory at the Ring Hop. Or maybe giving her a firm handshake.

Illustration for November, Sphinx Calendar, 1965
I liked this cartoon more than my girl did.

My roommate was intensely training for the Ring Hop Sword Drill performance as I was looked forward to taking my girl to the big dance. Of all the spit and polish moments of a year, the Ring Hop was unique. The big dance was the Saturday after the ceremony when seniors received their class rings. Everyone was in their formal wear, the cadets wearing full dress salt and pepper (white pants/cadet-grey, multi-buttoned–up blouse). The lights went dark as spotlights reflected on the polish of the field house court floors and highlighted the golden replica of the ring, big enough to walk through with your date.

With severe precision, the fifteen-minute Drill ended in a double line of arching swords, forming a path in front of the big ring. (This was the moment I tried to capture for *The Shako* cover.) Then each graduating senior escorted his date though the ring and arched swords.

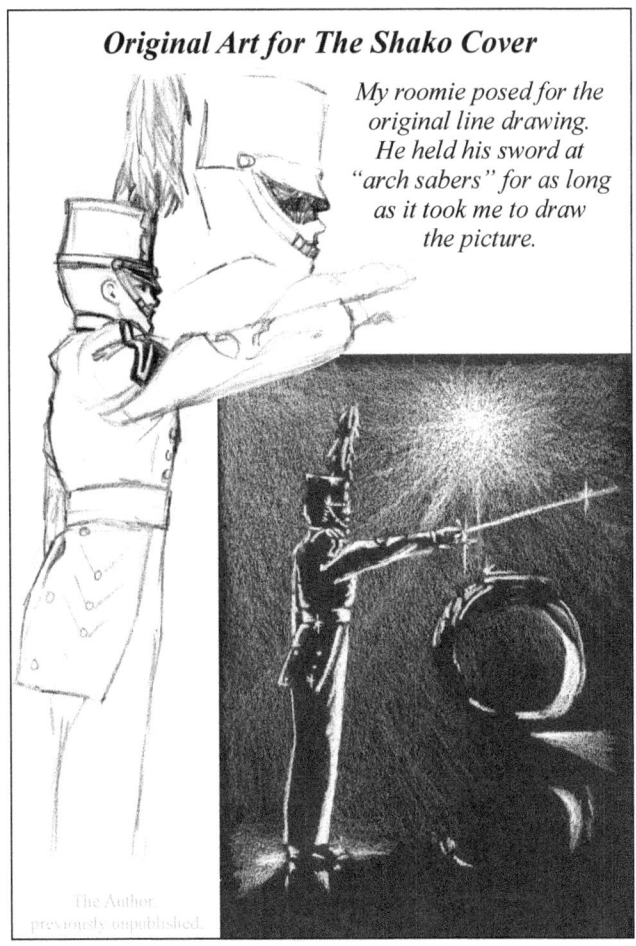

Original Art for The Shako Cover

My roomie posed for the original line drawing. He held his sword at "arch sabers" for as long as it took me to draw the picture.

The Author
previously unpublished.

It was typical for seniors to indulge a kiss at the appropriate moment in the ring and also for girls who personally knew individuals in the Drill to dish out pecks on cheeks as they walked beneath the swords. I accept responsibility for any distortions in the depictions of these traditions, whether in *The Sphinx* calendar or in *The Shako*. What I drew may not have happened – but *could* have.

CID SCENES

by ed west

(The) Shako,
Homecoming, 1964

The title of the 1965 calendar was "12/240." On the cover were three wretches walking tours. The title was derived from a term that represented a life sentence. Other than dismissal from school, the most severe punishment in *The Blue Book* available for the Commandant to award was 120 tours, associated with six months restriction to campus while those tours were being walked. Cadets referenced the life sentence as "six-and-a-hundred-and-twenty." In those days, "12/240" was an entire calendar year. Shot.

Illustration for March, Sphinx Calendar, 1965

One of my favorite images was for the month of March and the uplifted Spirit of Spring. March was a time of release from winter misery and the dawn of a new season of hope: recognition, promotion, graduation and furlough. The month was represented by a fine, uniformed specimen being admired by a lovely miss and a noble dog, accompanied by his date. I have been asked what was the attraction of girls and dogs to cadets. I don't know and by experience, I learned not to inquire about such things. Perhaps we looked like manly fire plugs.

9. – BARRACKS ADMINISTRATION

9.25. VISITORS IN BARRACKS

a. Civilians: No civilians may enter barracks unless escorted by an officer or cadet.

b. No visitor shall be taken into the barracks at any time without proper authority.

The Commandant considered women to be civilians in those days, so their presence among us was regulated. Pets were prohibited, but there was no regulation in *The Blue Book* concerning dogs, lizards or hamsters living in the barracks. (A specimen or more of each of these co-habited with us in one or more of the barracks. Almost certainly specimens unknown to me were also enlisted on the zoological muster roll.)

I don't remember when I first became aware that there was a Renfru where I lived, but he showed up in my art in the fall of 1964. I assumed he wasn't a civilian, because civilians in the barracks without proper authority were not permitted. As far as I know, he wasn't a pet of anyone, particulary. But I assumed that he must have one or more enablers among the inmates. I never knew who they were. Maybe Renfru was the pet owner.

16. – CONDUCT

16.04.(v.)

Pets: No cadet or group of cadets will have a pet in barracks.

(The) Shako.
Spring, 1965

Renfru and his pet cadet.

The dog of my art was an inside joke, appreciated by those unfortunates who lived in Number 3 barracks. His name was "Renfru."

25. INSPECTION

25.02. – SATURDAY MORNING INSPECTION OF BARRACKS:

a. Formal room inspection will be made on Saturday.

16.04. GENERAL RULES GOVERNING CONDUCT

m. Food in Rooms: The prolonged presence of food in cadet rooms is prohibited. All food brought into rooms will be consumed prior to the next morning room inspection.

I don't know what happened to Renfru on Saturday morning inspections (SMI). But there must have been a plan and perhaps even a central planning committee to store and distribute the necessary kibble. Perhaps the committee itself consumed all the dog food remaining on Friday evening after parade. Or maybe they delivered it to the homeless mongrels who haunted the back door of the mess hall.

(The) Shako,
Graduation, 1964

Aha---- hidden peanuts, S.M.I.

Number 3 barracks was my home. It seemed natural for the dog to be glad to see me when I returned from school. But by the end of the semester, Renfru was more than just a fellow sufferer. He was the dorm mother I never knew and through my cartoons in *The Shako,* his notoriety increased because of new construction at the main gate. The Corps had learned that this was a "gate house" for a provost marshal and a new layer of authority for our lives. A retired Marine officer had been engaged to oversee campus security and he needed an office for his operations. More on this, later.

Prior to this time, campus security was the responsibility of the cadet guard, a rotating annoyance enjoyed by almost every one of all classes. A guard office was in the arched wall of each barracks sally port. It was always occupied by a guard member and was valued by the residents of the condominium because it was where the closest public phone was located.

The Cadet Guard

16. – CONDUCT

16.04. GENERAL RULES GOVERNING CONDUCT:

z. Respect for the Guard: All cadets will show respect for members of the guard. Disrespect toward a member of the guard is a serious offense.

The commandant distributed guard duty to almost all cadets in the four classes in a rotation through each academic year. The formation of "Guard mount" occurred daily on the quadrangle of Number 2 barracks and included a personal inspection by the Officer of the Day (OD.) The freshman in the formation who most impressed this senior cadet officer was designated "Colonel's Orderly."

The Colonel's Orderly (CO) wore a distinguishing arm band. For twenty-four hours, his sole duty was to be on call by the regimental commander. (This meant he usually had nothing to do.) It was easy for the CO to think he was pretty hot stuff for the moment. But he was Cinderella on a count-down to midnight.

I didn't really look forward to guard duty. But it was a break in the routine and excused me from classes and formations. When I was on guard duty my senior year, I was the Junior Officer of the Day (JOD). I drove a

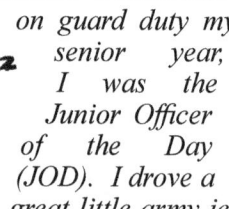

It means I'm the sharpest freshman on campus, Sir.

*great little army jeep around campus after **Taps** until dawn and carried the keys to the kingdom on my sword belt. Mom would have been proud of me.*

1 & 3, *(The) Shako*, Spring, 1965; 2, *(The) Shako*, Graduation, 1963

Guard duty occurred for me every few months. I didn't mind the job as a freshman because it was a time of eating three meals without any harassment. The one moment of "duty" as a knob I recall well was serving as a lookout for uninvited Tactical Officers who occasionally prowled around the galleries. If one from the dark side slipped into the barracks, my duty was to give fair warning to various miscreants who were in a moment of not abiding by *The Blue Book*.

On such occasions of alarm, I would stand in the middle of the quadrangle and, like Paul Revere, robustly call out "Phone call for Johnny Robinson." Those with the need to know, knew that there was no Johnny Robinson in the 3rd Battalion. This was the equivalent of an American sailor at Pearl Harbor hearing and understanding the meaning of the message *"Tora! Tora! Tora!"* It occurs to me that the tacs were never curious as to why Cadet Robinson always seemed to receive a call just as they entered Number 3 barracks. Of course, stranger things than this happened at my home with a view of the Ashley marsh.

When I was a junior on guard duty, I supervised the raising and lowering of the garrison flag. The parade ground flag pole was directly beyond the sally port of Number 3 barracks, so the 3rd Battalion cadet guard had this duty. On my watch, the flag never touched the ground and was never raised upside down. If it happened on anyone else's watch, I probably wouldn't have known – the poor sad sack responsible would have been gone by *Taps*.

I was a Citadel cadet for four years and have the diploma somewhere to prove it. But I never felt like I was a member of the Corps of Cadets. Even as an upperclassman, it seemed that I was an observer rather than a participant, like a civilian reporter embedded in a military combat unit.

I simply couldn't quite believe that there was a place on the planet where what happened at The Citadel, happened. It was like one of those annoying dreams in which you *know* that you are dreaming and wish you would wake up so it would go away. I dreamed away those four years and so, coped. (I have learned from classmates at reunions that all of us were coping, each in his own way – some by resistance, and some by prayer, or therapy, or beer.)

(The) Shako,
Graduation, 1964

THE CORE OF CADETS

In a time other than physical training, study periods, inspections, and parades during my junior year, I was the art editor for *The Shako*. A short story by Pat Conroy, the widely celebrated southern author who inherited the mantle of William Faulkner, was published that year; I was the illustrator. I knew Pat Conroy as an underclassman and a basketball jock. But in 1964 on *The Shako* staff, he was a writer and I did the illustrations for published stories.

I mention Pat Conroy because, in that time and place, he was to writing as I was to art: we both tended to exercise right brain operations in a left brain culture. Also, we both caused some heartburn in *The Shako* to college authorities and we both became better at our respective trades with time.

16. – CONDUCT

16.04. GENERAL RULES GOVERNING CONDUCT

x. Publications: Any authorized publications, such as the annual and the college paper, will be issued under the responsible supervision of a cadet editor who will submit all material to a specifically appointed committee of the facilty (*sic*) for approval before it is sent to the printer

I was aware that all of my literary and artistic expressions were subject to censorship. But it was in my junior year that I actually had a conversation with two of the luminaries who comprised the "specially appointed committee of the facilty (*sic*)." It was just another rigged trial for me when it happened. But years later, I learned that my encounter was historic.

Unlike Conroy, I had long made my peace with my *alma mater* when I received a phone call from Colonel D. D. Nicholson, who wanted to confirm an incident which involved Colonels, Generals and me. Col. Nicholson, the assistant to General Clark when I was a cadet, told me that he was writing a book which would be published by The Association of Citadel Men in 1994 titled, "A History of The Citadel: The Years of Summerall and Clark."

I remembered the Colonel from meetings of the Round Table. He was a pleasant, reserved Marine officer whose posture always seemed to be under the influence of a broom handle laced to his spine. Colonel Nick called because he was involved from the administration end in an incident of 1965 that involved me from the cadet end. He wanted to know my side of the story. He told me his end – then I gave him an earful.

The incident centered on the cadet reaction to news of the provost marshal office to be constructed at the main gate. We were told that our newest oppressor, Major Holliday, was actually a swell guy and that having an administrative provost marshal in a new guardhouse was a good idea. But there was an almost universally negative reaction in the Corps.

70

The historical moment of inquiry to which I contributed was ultimately described in Col. Nicholson's book which, on page 337 reads:

> *"The position of provost marshal was established to improve campus security. The cadets, however, naturally assumed that Major Holliday's primary mission was to intensify control of the Corps by the administration. These fears were dispelled by an announcement, approved by the president, which stated that the provost marshal 'would not be concerned with internal functions of the Corps of Cadets or in administering cadet discipline,' but not before an eight-page cartoon series depicting the provost marshal as an anti-cadet gestapo had been prepared for the spring 1965 edition of The Shako. Cadet Edward Hackett West... drew the cartoons to reflect the majority opinion within the Corps. West was persuaded by the dean of the college, Brigadier General James William Duckett, '32, to withdraw the cartoons."*

Over two decades later, as Colonel Nick and I spoke on the phone, I remember being amused that this awkward moment in my life was historic in the view of Colonels and Generals. (It never occurred to me that General Clark was involved, or that I had been "persuaded" of anything.) But mostly I remembered how my encounter with the highest levels of authority resulted in *Der Marchenmarshenschulen*, the literary wonder I consider to be the pinnacle of my covert journalistic revelation of truth about cadet life.

39. – REPORTING

39.03. ORDERED TO REPORT: A cadet ordered to report in person to an officer of the college will do so at the appointed time.

As I remember the incident (and I remember it as though it were an hour ago), I had returned to my little hole in the wall in Number 3 barracks from a chemistry lab to find an unsigned note on my desk. Such notes were usually delivered by the cadet guard. It was not good to find a note on your desk.

"See Gen. Duckett," the note read. That was for sure, not good.

Within a few minutes, I was knocking on the door of the academic dean of the school. I didn't recall ever having a conversation with General Duckett, but I knew that he and my uncle had been Citadel friends about thirty years earlier.

"Come in."

I did, saluted, and spoke: "Cadet West, reporting as ordered, sir."

The dean was holding papers which I recognized as my cartoon article on the new provost and guardhouse, submitted for publication. He almost smiled; then, in a fatherly tone asked, "Ed, did you write this?"

'Ed?' Nobody called me 'Ed.' I was no longer sure that my mother still called me "Ed." I glanced at the papers and answered, "Yes, sir."

"You know we can't publish this," he said, possibly sympathetically.

"Yes, sir."

"Do you want this, or do you want me to keep it?"

"You may keep it, sir."

"That is all," he said. I saluted, faced about, closed the door as I left, and that was all.

Well, not exactly. Back in my hole in the wall, I had my private reaction: "They can't do that," said I to Ed.

Not surprisingly, my familiar dark demons were already fomenting a counter-attack. I was in a second-year modern language course of German as a junior and my spirit-friends informed me of a plan in a tongue known only to us.

I would write an illustrated, unvarnished, literary triumph about what it was like to be a cadet in the barracks in the '60s. In order to pass the college censors, it would be in "pig-German," a fractured version of the honorable language of Deutschland. I had learned to appreciate this affectation of English words strung together to look like German words through a cartoon series in the *Saturday Evening Post* magazine.

The title of my cartoon-rich *wunderyarn* would be titled, "Der Marchenmarshenschulen" (the Marching School in the Marsh) and co-star *das renfruhoundenpetzen*. With its condescending sub-title, referencing South Carolina's perpetual senator, Strom Thurmond, the editor's introduction to my essay follows:

DER MARCHENMARSHENSCHULEN
(Der Lernenscholarfinkenbilder dem Thurmondsecessher Staaten)

EDITOR'S NOTE: *This is an account taken directly from the annals of the German journal "Was is Das, Schulen oder Gutentimenhellenraisen?" (Literally, "What's What in American Colleges and Universities.") The transcript has been left in the original German and may be translated by sight only (refer to Memorandum No. I, Foreign Language Dept., The Citadel.) A glossary at the end would probably only confuse things.*

With this deliberately intimidating beginning, the pig-German-captioned cartoons on seven pages awaited the discriminating reader's translation. Perhaps the less discriminating (such as my tormentors in the Commandant's Department) would search for amusing evil elsewhere. I had only a forlorn hope that it would be published in the spring edition of *The Shako*.

I was not surprised that, two weeks after I submitted this new and improved effort, I found a note again on my desk after chem lab: "See Col. ...," it read. This particular Colonel was the gatekeeper to the throne room.

Now the Colonel was not the dean. General Duckett was a *bona fide* academic. On the other hand, cadets thought that the Colonel served as a dud torpedo for the Godfather with all the stars. In my contacts with him, his manner seemed abrupt and his insight variable. (Some of my associates speculated that the Colonel's Sherman tank turret took a glancing round from a German 88mm in the North African Campaign.) Whatever his story, he wasn't the dean and I was optimistic about my prospects in the next interview:

"Cadet West reporting as ordered, sir."

In the dramatic court room manner of Perry Mason, he extended my familiar manuscript with cartoons toward me: "West – you write this?"

I glanced at the evidence with appropriate concern and said cheerfully, "Yes, sir."

38. – REPORTS, OFFICIAL

38.01. GENERAL: Reports either oral or written made by cadets in connection with official performances of duty are accepted as fact (or are to the best knowledge or belief of the cadet reporting) by the person receiving the report. Official reports are matters of personal honor.

"Looks like it's all in a foreign language to me."

Solicitously, I leaned a little forward to inspect the evidence more carefully. "Yes, sir," I replied thoughtfully. "It does appear that way, sir."

"Anything offensive in this?"

Cheerful again, I responded, "Gee, I don't think so, sir."

And so, "Der Marchenmarshenschulen" was featured in the spring edition of *The Shako*. I became a cult celebrity to certain marginalized acquaintances of mine and later I made the history book, although I have always thought that the full story was more compelling than Colonel Nick's account.

Der Marchenmarshenschulen

Der Marchenmarshenschulen was published in the spring issue of The Shako. I composed this screed in a moment of passion. After twenty months as a stone statue in Commandant Pygmalion's studio, I had finally come to life. I now realize that the seven pages of cartoons captioned in pig-German were my opus that would lead to my troubled retirement as an honorable member of the underground. Here are three samples for those who enjoy gazing at modern art and wondering, "What was it with this guy?"

Der Studenter at "El Cid" ist nicht ein Studenter. Der Studenter ist ein Marchenscheinenpullenclassmater.

Ein Marchenscheinenpullenclassmater und das renfruhoundenpetzen

Denn der Schulenday ist kaput und der "Cadet" playzen ein Leggenbreakerrearenkickennamencallenintramuralisch....

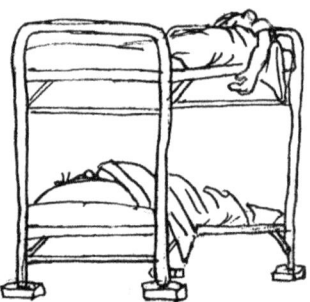

Der "cadets" uppencleaner der Room.

Der Leggenbreakerrearenkickennamencallenintramuralisch.

(The) Shako, Spring, 1965

The spring issue of *The Shako* was out in time for Corps Day, which was particularly memorable. That was the weekend I "pinned" my sweetheart, now a sophomore at Furman University. The cloisonné pin was the size of a tie tack. It comprised a Citadel shield with swords and had a miniature pewter numeral "66" attached to it. I don't know what it meant to her. For me, it sealed a commitment to a shared future, as far as that might go.

Actually, beyond securing my love life, I had no clear idea about my future in the spring of 1965. The conflict in Vietnam dominated the news. My family's plan to move to Vietnam only a few months earlier had collapsed because of the escalation. The U.S. Government had moved my father alone to an apartment in Saigon; my mother and brothers were now living in Charleston. They were separated from me only by the toothless lion in Hampton Park and the lock on the sally port gate.

I was among the minority of cadets who "turned down" an ROTC officer candidate contract. My highly ranked roommate was the kind of man the Army wanted for combat officers. He had signed an Army contract and would be a 2nd lieutenant when he graduated in 1966, just as I would be prime meat for the draft. Every cadet knew, contract or otherwise, that tickets to Vietnam were ours, sooner or later. But then a contrary thought began to percolate as a result of tinkering inside a cat.

Most seniors had to submit an acceptable senior essay to meet graduation requirements. For many in science majors this would often be a report on a months-long research project, including laboratory investigation and archival documentation. A preliminary proposal for this required essay was supposed to be approved before the end of the junior year.

Having spent most of a semester slicing and shredding the remains of a cat in comparative anatomy class, it occurred to me that the work would be easier if I had an illustrated manual to guide my dissection. So I submitted a senior essay proposal to devise a manual for the job, illustrated by the author. With no true research involved, this was uncharted territory for a senior essay in a science major. But the proposal was approved and from this, I first considered that I could become a medical illustrator for a career (assuming the variables of Vietnam worked out.)

Without much thought, I asked enough questions to determine that a master's degree in the subject was only offered in a few universities; one of these was the Medical College of Georgia. I had the science grades to be a contender but I would need to submit a portfolio of my art as part of an application. My art had been a hit among my fellow lowbrows in the barracks. But cartoon drawings of Renfru were hardly something to submit for a master's level art degree. So I scrambled to gather art from my attic at home and went for an interview in Augusta.

I was in uniform for the occasion and was treated with respect. But I found that I was one of over a hundred applicants competing for two slots. (The escalating war had apparently encouraged many draft-eligible draftsmen to seek a graduate education.) Virtually all of the other applicants had spent the last few years in art colleges, preparing their portfolios. It was nice that I was a science student – but they were looking for artists and I was clearly not in the competition.

Meanwhile, for reasons unknown, I decided to join many of my pre-med co-laborers and take the national Medical College Admission Test. I reassured my friends I was uninterested in a medical career. I did not study for it and I honestly don't even know what I scored on it. But I took it and eventually, that mattered.

> **The Citadel Code** "earnestly commended to all cadets":
> To make the college better by reason of my being a cadet.
> – Mark W. Clark, President

Later into spring, I was chosen by the three under classes of M Company to serve as company honor representative for the next year. Meanwhile, the Director of Cadet Activities urged me to accept the position of editor-in-chief of *The 1966 Sphinx*. Selection as honor representative had been a goal of mine since I was a freshman. But I wasn't looking for the stress of the yearbook to be added to my senior courses, which included Physical Chemistry. My fatalistic outlook that spring led me to accept the Director's direction with an attitude of "*What difference could one more thing make?*"

My attitude seemed only realistic at the time. Perhaps I wasn't truly at peace inside, but I had come to a truce within myself. I now realize that this private part of my life had been influenced over the recent months by my experiences in chapel services as a member of the Sunday Color Guard.

The chapel was of a classic "Latin Cross" design with a nave containing pews along a central aisle. This seating area was large enough to hold the hundreds of cadets who attended Protestant services each Sunday. Symmetrical smaller wings perpendicular to this area – "transepts" – provided seating for faculty, staff and visitors near the altar and pulpit. Above the broad porch entrance outside, the stone was inscribed with a verse from Ecclesiastes in capital letters:

"REMEMBER NOW THY CREATOR IN THE DAYS OF THY YOUTH."

Most Sunday mornings of my first two years had been spent in Episcopal services with formations which were earlier in the morning and far less ostentatious. But I was aware of the glamor of the formations for the main Protestant services. On Sunday mornings, the Protestant cadets marched in dress uniforms across the wide parade ground to the chapel from the barracks, company guidons snapping in the breeze. The sleepy young men made their parents and girlfriends proud as they piously filed up the stone steps, removed their hats, passed down the center aisle and filled the nave, remaining at attention by their pews.

The cadets of the Sunday Color Guard then shifted the focus of everyone as we entered with the *Stars and Stripes* and the blue *Palmetto Flag* of the Corps of Cadets. The job of the color guard inside was to place these two large flags in their stands on the stage in front before the service began and then, when the service closed, to recover the flags. The trick for the guard was to do our job silently. The drill was complicated by the necessity of removing and replacing military hats inside the chapel.

The uniform hat is an individual's "cover" in military jargon. Military etiquette requires those in uniform to always wear a cover when outside and to remove their hats as they enter a building. Those cadets who broke ranks and entered ahead of the color guard removed their hats routinely. But the entering color guard was still on duty and facing a conundrum regarding authority, respect and covers.

The Citadel dress hat has a brass palmetto-tree-pin prominently displayed on its front crown. On the head of a cadet (so, physically above him), the insignia represents the authority (the S.C. state government) which "covers" him. For the members of the color guard, the authority of the state still "covered" us as we performed our duties inside the chapel for The Military College of South Carolina. The difficulty was that our duty was performed at an interface between the authority of a human institution and the divine authority who was being worshipped in the Sunday morning service. When respecting the nation, the state and the school, a cover was required; when rendering to God, "*the things that are God's*," we were properly uncovered.

On the Sunday Color Guard, my position in the formation was beside one of the flag-bearers. When we entered the chapel two-by-two, the two men with the colors advanced up the steps to the stage in front. I was immediately behind them. As the color bearers were positioning on the stage, I was wheeling at the front pew, leading the others to reach our positions. My place was at the very end of the first pew, directly in front of the pulpit.

In weekly drills, we practiced saluting in slow-motion in unison, guided by our peripheral vision. Then we practiced silently sitting or standing as one and reverently removing and replacing our hats. The commander initiated each of these personal actions by an almost imperceptible tipping forward into our line of peripheral sight. His position was on the far end of the pew, down the line from me. The other guard members lined up between us. The silence, precision, unity and exaggerated deliberateness of all these elements of ceremony were designed to show profound respect.

At my end of the pew, the right transept of the chapel interfaced with the nave. The pews in this area were facing mine and the front row was for the President and dignitaries. On Sundays, as I led the line of the detail along the front row pew, I was stepping directly toward General Clark. He was standing and facing me like a pillar, just beyond the end of my pew, six feet distant. In my years as a cadet, I had had only a few, brief conversations with him and his constellations of shining stars. On Sunday mornings, I doubt that he recognized me. But I was sure that he saw me. When he looked straight ahead, there was nothing but me to see.

As for me, seated or standing, I was at "attention" for an hour in the chapel. Even though my eyes were directed straight ahead toward the pulpit, I sensed the General in my peripheral vision. Looking straight forward (as was expected and proper) I couldn't see him. But I knew he saw me and was watching. I do not recall making an important mistake as the General watched, Sunday after Sunday. In fact, I am certain I *would* remember because I was so aware of being watched in those moments.

I think passing beneath the admonition to remember my Creator, then the solemn repetitions under the General's inspection each Sunday, had an effect on me. By the end of my junior year, I profoundly feared the Lord. I remembered Him as the One who continuously watched me. The day would come when my reverence for God and His Word would permanently replace *The Blue Book* as the guide of my life.

The summer before my senior year was a season of decision. I had spent the previous two summers in rehab, finding recovery as a counselor in a Pocono Mountains camp for boys. Those were good days, free of the reality at *der Marchenmarshenschulen*. But I was 21 years old and only a year away from a degree and the draft. What then? That's when my father came home from Vietnam with an answer.

Physical Chemistry and my senior essay loomed as the last big academic hurtles to overcome. I knew that Honor Committee work and the yearbook would demand more time than I could afford to spend away from my academics. As a partial solution, I stayed with my Charleston family to attend summer school and face the difficult chemistry course when I had no other distraction.

As contrasted with the hands-on, in-your-face, authoritarian control of The Citadel, my parents had been relatively laid back in their use of authority with me. I now see that this was largely determined by who the three of us were. My parents clearly admired each other and were mutually supportive in issues with their four boys. They lived their private lives by the same standards that they taught us. For whatever reason, I was generally compliant and teachable; I also enjoyed their conversation and company. In maturity, I appreciate the golden advantage of my childhood.

Above Illustrations *(The) Shako,* Spring, 1964

My father did not often speak directly into my life. He and my mother seemed to believe in me and had confidence in my decision-making. From my end, I had a high regard for their thoughts and it was my policy to listen to them. So that summer, my father was asking about the year I had just completed and about my plans. He unexpectedly took my nebulous answer as an opportunity to ask why I didn't apply for medical school. I took his question as advice and my application was out with the August mail.

14. – COMMAND AND STAFF

14.01. CADET OFFICERS AND NONCOMMISSIONED OFFICERS:

a. Appointments: Cadet officers and noncommissioned officers are appointed by the Commandant of Cadets with the approval of the President. The basis of appointment will be military and academic proficiency combined with character qualifications.

c. Duties and responsibilities: Cadet officers and noncommissioned officers are responsible for maintaining discipline, for instructing those placed under their control, and for setting a soldierly example at all times. It is the duty of every cadet officer and noncommissioned officer to support the authority of his superior and to assert his own authority whenever a breach of discipline makes it necessary at any place and under all circumstances.

When I returned to the barracks that fall, my roommate from my junior year was company commander. He and I occupied a large corner room, along with two other ranking seniors. The four of us had been good friends from early days. We four returned early for cadre week training and then were active in training freshmen as they arrived. But our minds were elsewhere: we were seniors and the end was in sight. I was particularly busy organizing the yearbook staff and outlining that project for the year.

In those first days in September of cadre training, I truly felt like a senior cadet. There were no classes, no freshmen, no drill, and my only associates were ranking upperclassmen. Daytime schedules were filled with meetings; meals were optional, and evenings were free until *Taps*. Conversations over pizza at *LaBrasca's* near Hampton Park with the big men on campus were relaxing and helpful for me as a writer and editor.

In one memorable moment, a regimental staff officer (and classmate) stroked the gold strap on his garrison cap and said, almost romantically, "This is everything." I gathered we were speaking of the meaning of his rank. My hat had a gold strap too, but my relationship with it wasn't as intense.

As I came to know many of my classmates with high rank, I also knew that my roommate should have been ranked among them. He was company commander because it was a particularly demanding job and he was a natural leader. Also, M Company seniors who were qualified and available to fill necessary rank slots were scarce. Tom accepted the bump downward without complaint and I admired him for this attitude. In my view, he proved to be an exceptional company commander.

I was ranked third among the rising seniors in my company. This ranking had led to a late spring interview with I-don't-remember-who about what my expectations might be as a rising cadet officer. My ambivalence about rank must have come out in the discussion. The only part of the evaluation I remember occurred during a drill practice on the parade ground. Someone was listening critically then as I called the imaginary battalions to attention. If I had gotten the job of the person who did that on Fridays, I would have been the regimental adjutant my senior year. (Imagine that!)

I had neither the military record, the time, nor the interest to be higher ranked. My obligations of conscience as honor representative would be enough stress. When assignments were eventually posted, I learned that I would be M Company executive officer. As exec, my job was mostly administrative and acting as second-string quarterback for Tom when he had circumstantial conflicts as company commander. This did not happen often.

21. – EXPLANATIONS

c. All written explanations will be submitted before the next supper formation following the posting of the delinquency list.

21.02. HOW SUBMITTED:

When a written explanation is made it will be submitted with the appropriate delinquency list to the Commandant of Cadets by the Cadet First Sergeant. Company Executive Officers will review all explanations for clarity, brevity, pertinence and correctness.

My most time-consuming job as company exec was the almost daily reviewing of the written responses originating in the company from cadets to reports of their misconduct. These official response letters were addressed to the Commandant. Responses in "writing" (actually typed by pecking along on a typewriter which each of us had in our rooms) were known as "ERWs." The term abbreviated the title of the letter: "Explanation of Report, Written."

When the company massed for parade, my place in formation was in the last rank, ostensibly to maintain alignment and watch for mischief in the rear. The company caboose was the haunt of senior privates and I learned their ways firsthand through regular, casual conversations as we marched along together. It was these experiences with both sides of the rank system that gave me a broader point of view in my contributions for publications.

Maybe

(The) Shako, Spring, 1964

From my position in the last rank of the company, the feathered plumes of the officers in front seemed to come alive in a breeze. I couldn't see much from the rear and I don't know for sure - maybe they really did.

Rank was necessary and possibly a good thing. A higher status would train me in the effective use of authority but risked relationships. Subordinate roles were inevitable for many and useful for learning submission, passive aggression or victimhood. We were a military family. The conflict for Citadel cadets between friendships and getting the job done was the classic, eternal conflict of siblings and armies.

Soon after the year began, it was obvious that the old order had changed. General Clark retired that fall. His successor was General Harris, a veteran with a distinguished record but not a WW2 giant. He seemed to want to reshape the place through the Commandant's Department. By this intention, he determined to correct misinterpretations of *The Blue Book*, particularly pertaining to freshmen. So when the new fourth classmen arrived, the knobs were often chaperoned by tacs from the Commandant's Department with unannounced drop-ins by various Colonels and an occasional General. It was a walking-on-eggshells time for the cadre in the barracks.

A nothing incident drips in the basement of my memories as I write of my senior year. After a supper that fall, there was a football pep rally when a serious loss of decorum was briefly tolerated. Such Thursday evening moments amok were authorized for purposes of launching the football team into Saturday's contest.

81

Rallies were held on the quad of Number 2 barracks and if anyone was in-charge, it was our male cheerleaders. These worthies were usually widely popular senior privates who had surprisingly found useful, authorized work. (Our class president was one of them.) Sometimes the Boo, our Assistant Commandant, would stand at the rail of the 2nd division gallery, peer down on the squalid mass on Basilica Square, and give his blessing to the manifested school spirit. For the great unwashed below, noise and chaos were our marching orders, empty trash cans were our instruments, and toilet paper rolls were our pompons to be launched with the team.

Status is...
a roll of toilet paper
at a pep rally.

(The) Shako,
Fall, 1965

A uniformity of uniforms was optional at rallies. At the one I am recalling, I was unfortunately still in uniform, including my black necktie. My tie seemed to be standard with a four in hand knot, but was actually a clip-on, held in place by a covert, paperclip-like metal collar stay. With this arrangement, I saved a few seconds in getting dressed each morning because I didn't have to wrap and tie the knot repeatedly. Also, since most of it was tucked into my shirt, I had cut off the unseen lower half of the tie.

When I returned to my room after this particular rally, I first noticed that I had lost my clip-on tie to some anonymous assailant in the roiling stew on the quadrangle. I had no spare tie – I had no reason to need one until this moment. I asked around but it seems no one else had one to loan me. I went to bed with no solution for the expectations of *Reveille*.

Photograph from the author's collection

0630hrs Breakfast Formation at der Marchenmarshenschulen

The one reliably forgiving formation was the first one of the day. The highest ranking cadets may have looked sharp, but in my four years, I can't recall actually seeing one before I had a cup of coffee.

1. – THE CHARACTER OF THE COLLEGE

1.02. GUIDING PRINCIPLES:

c. Punctuality: A cadet will be punctual at every duty and appointment, whether he is summoned by a general call (steel, bugle, etc.), obliged to watch the time for himself, or otherwise.

I was never "pulled" (reported) late for a breakfast formation – regardless of how I looked. But for years after I graduated, a recurring dream that I was late for formation troubled my sleep - not to mention, my wife, who I would sometimes awaken as I unconsciously wrestled down my demons and raced to the quad. (BTW - my girl became my wife in 1967 and, for better or worse, remains so.)

The next day, I stood in formation tieless. I was a senior officer with a zipped-up jacket, so no one noticed. I made it through breakfast, counting on the fact that no one ever noticed anything at breakfast. Then I spent the hour before classes violating *The Blue Book* (regulation 16.04., c.) unsuccessfully:

16. – CONDUCT

16.04. GENERAL RULES GOVERNING CONDUCT:

c. Borrowing and Lending: The borrowing or lending of equipment, uniforms, wearing apparel, or other article or property, public or private is prohibited.

My first class was a laboratory and my classmates included high ranked seniors, including a few on different staffs. *Maybe I can make it to the Cadet Store across campus after class*, I thought.

41. – SERVICES

41.02. THE CADET STORE: The Cadet Store is operated by the Quartermaster for the convenience of the cadets. Clothing and equipment needed by cadets may be obtained through approved requisitions charged to the cadet's account or by cash purchase.

But then it happened: "Where's your tie?" asked a laboratory co-worker on staff.

(The) Shako,
Spring, 1965

LEADER: 3ʳᵈ Battalion Staff's the best, to hell with the rest!
ALL: Amen, Amen!

The award for "improper uniform" was "5, 10 and 2" (five demerits, ten confinements and two weeks restriction to campus.) I thought my tale of the night before might help, but it didn't. I hoped for mercy, but I deserved what I received. So much for seeing my girl that month. That was how life worked.

As 1965 matured, the alarm in the barracks over the presence of the new provost marshal had diminished to occasional moments of commentary in the back ranks. I certainly had gotten off my high horse as an editorial cartoonist and had begun to adapt to the new ways of authority. I used my cartoons to express my more mature attitude toward the realities of cadet life. This was the season that I produced my observations on the meaning of status from a cadet's point of view.

I see now that I wasn't defining status as cadet rank, but rather in terms of peer values. For instance, rank itself didn't necessarily imbue status in the cadet world. (This was certainly the case of my freshman view of sophomore corporals.) If there was status among cadets for those with higher rank, it was related to how the rank was expressed in the barracks culture. Also, some other things mattered more than rank.

All of us had been reduced to ground level in the first year. We were Lowcountry crabs stuck in a bucket, scraping against each other and wondering what became of the chicken neck. Status wasn't a thought then. Rather, it was *how do I get out of the bucket*? But then our individuality began to prove our unique differences. Truly, as freshmen we were a bunch of teenage siblings in a giant foster care family. The ideals of *The Citadel Code* were aspirations which for most of us were largely beyond reach.

> **The Citadel Code** "earnestly commended to all cadets": To revere God, love my country and be loyal to The Citadel.
>
> To be faithful, honest and sincere in every act and purpose and to know that honorable failure is better than success by unfairness or cheating.
>
> To perform every duty with fidelity and conscientiousness and to make DUTY my watchword. – Mark W. Clark, President

With too many oppressive rules and restrictions, we were mostly tolerating each other as we tried to stay alive and dreamed of a world beyond. The responsible adults in "Mark Clark's Home for Unwed Fathers," seemed to enforce rules irregularly: sometimes severely and sometimes not at all. If we survived and reached the status of upperclassmen, it was because we learned critical survival tricks. Meanwhile, interpersonal conflict arose from daily choices between maintaining relationships, upholding standards and achieving objectives, as we suppressed anger and despair.

Perhaps the most important psychological accomplishment of my plebe year was learning to successfully cope with the feelings of stress. Coping - putting up with people and/or circumstances - is distinguished by the uncomfortable inner feelings of stress. If I could improve a circumstance to some extent by cleverness and competency, I did. I usually accepted people as they were; when they were odious, I could hope they would move on, one way or another. I was trained to override expressing feelings. It was only one more step to no longer admit the feelings.

For me, socialization made a major contribution to my coping. When I was a freshman, I socialized with fellow-sufferers assigned to my company. In those days, taller cadets were assigned to the companies positioned furthest from the reviewing stand at parade; the shorter guys filled in the companies in the middle of the parade formation. The idea was that perspective from the General's central position on the parade field would give the illusion of a uniform leveling across the companies. The arbitrariness of height to justify the arranging of companionships for eighteen-year-olds under stress is obvious.

An important part of my personal way of coping was to find humor in the crazy, the outrageous and the ironic. I drew for myself. But I really felt like I had made a contribution when my cartoons made a friend laugh, too. It seemed to me that there was something called "cadet humor" which was sardonic and crass. Cadet humor was not necessarily pervasive across the corps. But it was prevalent enough to wake up my muse in the middle of the night and compel me to sketch an idea to ink in tomorrow.

Like the individual cadets, the companies and the battalions tended to have their own reputations within the Corps. For instance, during my years, F Company was known as "F Troop." The name, which originated from a TV comedy featuring fouled up western cavalrymen, was cheerfully (proudly?) accepted by the guys in F Company. The 4th Battalion seemed to be more relaxed than the others; a speak-easy operated underneath the floor of the battalion barracks in my years. These notions of differences among the units tended to persist year-to-year as one generation begat the next.

Perhaps it was stress that brought the Commandant into the mess hall for a verbal confrontation with the Corps in the fall of 1965. His concerns over the plebe system and associated upper class failures in observing *The Blue Book* compelled his visit during a noon meal. At the microphone, he spoke of recent history in the barracks from the viewpoint of the Generals and Colonels. Then he spoke of the contamination of standards and morale produced by certain cadet slackers and miscreants.

Above Illustrations *(The) Shako*, Spring, 1964

From his brief message, I was surprised to learn that I was operating among an "infinitesimal one percent" of upper class losers. I suspected that his admonishment was intended to inspire those who were beyond reproach. But as I personally digested his words, along with my pork chop, my reaction was surprise that the percentage was so low. Unhelpfully, I also vicariously enjoyed identifying with these unnamed misfits. I learned later that most of my friends reacted similarly.

I knew of no specific mishap that might have triggered the Commandant's evaluation that day. Neither did I know why he chose that day to unload. From a cadet's point of view, there always seemed to be a piece missing in making sense of the next thing to happen. There were patterns and routines that just always seemed to be true, whether or not they made sense. These mysteries swirled around me regardless of my insight or contributions, like *Little Egypt*, doing her famous *Dance of the Pyramids* for the Coasters.

But some things that made little sense were fixed as fact because I owned them personally. One of these realities was that in the fall of 1965, I knew I would someday be a doctor. Soon after I submitted my application for medical school and transcripts and recommendations had been received, I was interviewed by a professor of medicine. I only remember the doctor asking whether or not The Citadel football team was likely to beat Furman that year. (He was a Furman grad.)

A few weeks later, I received a letter from the registrar of the Medical College of South Carolina (modern MUSC) that I would be listed among the freshmen of the incoming Class of 1970. I had no idea why I was accepted while pre-med classmates were still chewing on their nails waiting to hear. My theory was that I would not have been accepted if the authorities thought I wouldn't be successful – so I knew I would.

Another reality that I accepted without understanding was the committed relationship between me and my girl. She was twenty-one when we kissed in the spotlighted circle at the Ring Hop. She had learned to accept the restrictions, interruptions and absences of my life as a cadet. From these interruptions, she also had a pretty solid idea of what our future of hospitals and midnight calls could look like. With all that, she didn't flinch. I thought of "my girl" whenever the *Temptations* sang our song (actually, *my* song.)

My junior year, I had been with her in a Charleston shop when she purchased a new blouse. The logo of the clothier was a lady bug. In the collar of her new shirt was a stick pin, a tiny lady bug painted red with black spots. I asked her for the pin and when she gave it to me, I stuck it on the front of my garrison hat. It was inconspicuous, but it could be seen at the line of the leather strap if someone were to look exactly there. There were no rules in *The Blue Book* about lady bugs, so I wore it afterwards to parades, inspections and wherever else my hat might venture. The ending of this story is coming.

Before Christmas of 1965, I had frequent interruptions in my routines. These hiccups were necessary because of the demands of obtaining group photographs for the yearbook which forced a dance between the barracks, the classrooms and picturesque sites. During this time, I developed a professional conversation with Lt. Colonel T. N. Courvoisie, the legendary "Boo" made famous by Pat Conroy's book. The Colonel was my contact in the Commandant's office for permission to miss the next required formation because of my work.

Many of my classmates knew the Boo well. Some had first made acquaintance with Boo as freshmen. (This was usually not good.) Some met him in a crisis, such as the unhappy misunderstanding that occurred between certain B Company jocks and some Charleston dandies at the Ark. The dust finally settled when the Boo arrived and spoke briefly with the Charleston police. "You take your lambs and I'll take mine," he said – or words to that effect.

The Boo was a maverick in the Commandant's Department. The recent changes seemed to have cramped his style by challenging his autonomy in administering military justice. Cadets in my circle had varying opinions of the Boo. A number of higher ranked cadets allied with the Commandant and his subordinate Tactical Officers. My roommate Tom didn't trust Boo from his junior year work on battalion staff. But I know many Citadel grads who would have never received their rings without the Colonel's intervention. In fact, in some cases, he paid for their rings.

I asked the Boo for mercy once – I was caught in bed the morning after an all-nighter with the Honor Committee. He promised to take care of it and I never heard from the report. Still, I served punishment awards twice as a senior. The first instance was when I lost my neck tie and involuntarily followed *The Blue Book* proscription against borrowing. The second time was directly and deliberately ordered by the Boo.

Above Illustrations (*The*) *Shako*, Spring, 1964

Photograph from the author's collection.

A Visit with the Assistant Commandant

LTC Thomas Nugent Courvoisie, the Assistant Commandant, was "the Boo" of legend. Sometimes we went to see him with our confessions. Sometimes he came seeking us as his lost lambs.

9. – BARRACKS ADMINISTRATION

9.09. DOORS UNLOCKED: The doors including screen doors of cadet rooms will not be locked or otherwise fastened so as to prevent entry at any time.

An unannounced visit by the Boo to your room was usually good for an adrenaline rush and a smile on his face didn't always mean that there was nothing to worry about. He seemed to like his job and most of us were glad he was there, especially when considering alternatives.

31. - OFFICIAL BUSINESS

31.02. OFFICIAL VISITS:

b. To the Commandant and Tactical Officers: Cadets should feel free to visit the Assistant Commandant during their free periods.

The Boo was our Mother Superior whose door was always open and as far as we knew, whose eyes never shut. If you returned to your room from class and found a note on your desk reading, "See me. – TNC," it was not considered necessarily a bad thing. It was more like drawing a "Chance" card in Monopoly.

The exposure of my egregious second failure as a senior cadet began innocently. I was requesting an excused absence for an unavoidable and reasonable extra-curricular demand. Boo approved my request and we two walked outside his office together, talking casually. I'll never forget standing beside him on the steps of Jenkins Hall as we scanned the campus across the parade ground.

"You've got a bug on your hat, bubba," he said quietly.

Nothing got by the Boo – cadets, bugs – nothing. I must have blinked. He squinted at me in the moment. Then, with the authority of his unique, rough brogue, he growled, "Let me see that bug!"

On the next company delinquency list were five demerits for, "West, E.H. – Bug on hat."

At this point in my writing, I have searched my copy of *The Blue Book* in vain to find a relevant regulation that I violated that day. I found nothing about bugs. Too late, I found this:

40. – RIGHTS OF REDRESS

40.01. SUBMISSION OF COMPLAINT: If any cadet shall consider himself wronged by another cadet or by any officer of the college, he may submit a complaint through the Commandant of Cadets to the President who will take further action as necessary to correct the wrong if an injustice had been done. Such complaints will be considered only when made within ten days after the occurrence of the alleged wrong.

The statute of limitations has expired, justice remains questioned, and I have determined to let it rest.

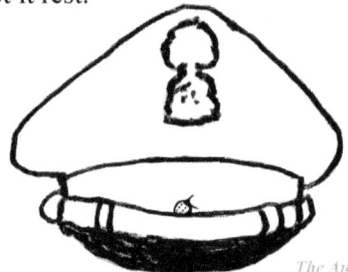

The Author, previously unpublished.

In the spring of 1966, the deadline for my senior projects was becoming very real. I had to submit the last third of the yearbook material to the publisher by the end of March, then my completed senior essay by the last of April. I had been hustling with the annual and met the date after several overnights in Mark Clark Hall, with the Boo's blessing.

34. – PASSES

34.08. CLASS "A" PASSES TO VISIT CHARLESTON:

a. With the approval of the President, The Citadel, all cadets, who are eligible, are granted a Class A pass to visit Charleston during the hours other than general leave from 1500 to 1755 hours.

My senior essay mostly comprised drawings of dissected cats in various states of disrepair. Most of my friends were hiring professional typists for the final edition of their essays. My mother was a stenographer at one point in her life and she offered to type the copy that was part of my project. It was spring, my family lived only a few blocks away, and Class A passes were not hard to secure. As my mother typed, I visited home fairly often, both in the afternoons and on other times of leave.

It was during this time that I would occasionally watch the new television comedy, *Hogan's Heroes*. The setting was a WW2 German prisoner of war camp (*Stalag 13*); the theme was the intrigues of a small group of allied POWs. These classic one-percenters were bonded as friends and determined to do their duty as prisoners: interrupt, resist and escape. Typical storylines would be the comical gyrations required to smuggle a partisan out of Germany, abscond with a Nazi codebook, or sabotage a critical dam.

The weekly stories of *Hogan's Heroes* were an allegory of my life. Today I see that they influenced my viewpoints of relationships, duty and purpose as a cadet. I had pressed some buttons in campus publications without actually setting off explosions (at least, there were no explosions directly attributed to me.) Now, as a senior, my time as the campus artist had come to a close.

By May, most of my obligations were fulfilled. The yearbook was in the print shop, my senior essay was on the department chairman's desk and my services were not required for the graduation issue of *The Shako*. This was fortunate because that was the issue that almost ended some Citadel careers.

30. – OFFENSES

30.01. OFFENSES CLASSIFIED:

c. Offenses of the First Class:

(4) Combining under any pretext whatever with other cadets or entering into any agreement with other cadets either in writing or orally with a view of procuring a redress of grievances or of violating or evading any regulation of the college; or joining with other cadets in disapprobation or censure of an officer or cadet or in doing any act contrary to the rules of good order and discipline.

Cadet Pat Conroy was the rising poetry editor in the spring of 1966 when two one-percenters submitted a frankly impertinent, personal challenge to the dignity of the Commandant and his subordinates. Their poem made it past the reviews of the editor and the facilty (*sic*). Its notoriety in the June *Shako* changed the magazine operation for years to come. I was grateful to have found a way out of *Stalag 13* before that dam burst.

In that same period, though, I did have a brush with the same kind of offense involving "disapprobation or censure" of a cadet. The individual was one of the highest ranked in my class, a member of the regimental staff. I had spoken with this person rarely, and then only briefly, before he approached me in Mark Clark Hall a few weeks before the yearbook was to be delivered. I must paraphrase what he said – it's been too long ago now. It was approximately, "You'd better not have any derogatory comments about me in *The Sphinx*." That was when I was glad I had abandoned ship with the other rats. I also confirmed the sobering thought that certain of my high-ranked classmates apparently did not share my sense of humor.

The irony of the moment was that if my indiscretion had been so beyond the pale that his good name was smudged in the annual, it was already a *fait accompli* – the yearbook was printed and ready for distribution. Another irony was that in a few days, he and I would be fellow graduates without any authority difference between us. He would be merely a former commander and I would be merely a fellow alumnus. (BTW - When I was a senior, it never occurred to me that I had a problem with the regimental staff or that the staff had a problem with me.)

I did well in May with my final exams and received an "A" on my senior essay. (The professor wrote that my typist received a "B." I don't think I told my mother of her grade.) I was with friends in a rented beach house when I received word that the yearbooks were on campus and being distributed. Graduation was still a few days away, but that was when I first felt like it was over.

As a senior, my social contacts had broadened. Through hours spent with cadets from across the Corps who served with me in extra-curricular activities, I truly had a rich social register. Still my heart was with the senior privates and their humble nobility, along with the seniors with rank who did their best to maintain friendships with their subordinates.

It was my joy to work alongside unremarkable and unrecognized cadets who were promoters of the school's goals and purposes. I suspect that many of them were unaware that this high ideal was commended to them by General Clark, even though they had signed a form that they had read his sentiment in *The Blue Book*. It was good for morale and the school that so many cadets were involved in the many extra-curricular jobs that needed attention.

I particularly appreciated the work of certain friends who did the scut work that produced *The 1966 Sphinx.* The hours we spent together helped broaden my understanding of how differently we processed the common circumstances and truths we witnessed and experienced together. From these shared memories of four years, I wrote the following in *The Sphinx* for all of us:

> *"The Citadel is a kaleidoscope of contrasts to the transient observer. The sudden release of deafening energy at retreat parade contradicts the ordered silence of a searching mind. 2,000 personalities lend sparkling color to a somber world of grey.*
>
> *When it all begins, you are the only guy in the world who knows you are alive. There is nobody to help you. Nobody to share a thought with...nobody. But the best part of beginning friendless is that it is impossible to end that way. In such a confining environment, fraternity is not a nicety – it is a necessity."*

When I wrote these words to introduce the *The 1966 Sphinx*, I thought I was writing a general truth. I realize now that I was still naïve about how each of us processed the four years. There are some classmates who passed through the same fire and yet would read these platitudes as "blah, blah, blah." Among these are ranking officers, senior privates, one-percenters and some who appreciated my cartoons.

(The) Shako,
Spring, 1964

93

(The) Shako.
Graduation, 1964

We were just practicing, sir.

Two More Books and the Whole Man

When I walked away from The Citadel with a diploma, I was walking toward General Clark's vision of "the whole man." He and his associates described this demigod in an ad in *The 1964 Sphinx*. Illustrated by inspiring, surreal images of transformed cadets, the ad reads:

THE CITADEL'S WHOLE MAN

The Citadel prides itself on its approach to educating the "whole man." This concept stresses that a cadet is trained not only academically and militarily but physically, morally, spiritually, and honorably.

For complete information address

GENERAL MARK W. CLARK, President

When I was a cadet in the '60s, I understood that if the school achieved success in my case, I would resemble, at some level, the "whole man" in the ad. (BTW, the whole man pictured in the ad had an uncanny resemblance to the regimental commander of that year.)

General Clark emphasized the whole man with the press and, on occasion, with us in speeches. The ideal of the whole man was that he lived a life that was beyond the confines of *The Blue Book* because he had mastered himself and was filled with virtue and insight. Not bad – but also, not likely true, at least on graduation day for the infinitesimal one-percenters who were walking away with diplomas along with me.

I doubt that I was much different in character the day before I received my diploma than I was after crossing the stage. Yet at my age now, I am certainly an improvement in many ways over the twenty-two year-old who joined his classmates as they all threw their hats up into the air that day. Now I attribute my progress toward becoming a whole man to two books beyond *The Blue Book of 1960.*

(The) Shako, Spring, 1965 The Author and Kevin Metzger

95

It seems as though my story should end with my graduation; in fact, that was my intention when I began. But the story of my life as a cadet is incomplete without dealing with how I am still becoming a whole man. Central to this transformation (which is a work in progress) has been the impact of the Honor Code on my life.

In 1962, there were two little books with blue paper covers hanging behind every room door in the barracks. On the hook with *The Blue Book of 1960* was *The Honor Manual of the Corps of Cadets*. Both books were blue, but one was much thicker. This was because it took a lot more paper to print everything that you could do wrong (or fail to do right). So, the 66 pages of rules in *The Blue Book* starkly contrasted with *The Honor Manual*'s ten pages and four simple rules. The Honor Code itself was stated in less than a page:

SECTION III – The Cadet Honor Code

4. *The Honor Code*: The Honor Code is a code of, by, and for The Corps of Cadets. The code states that a cadet does not lie, cheat, or steal. The code is the heart of the Honor System, and its purpose is to maintain honor and integrity within The Corps.

5. *Violations of the Code*: There are four, and only four, violations of the Honor Code. These are:

a. Lying: Making a false official statement. An official statement is defined as a statement, written or oral, made to a commissioned officer of the staff or of the faculty of the college, or a guard on duty, or any cadet required, in turn, to use the statement as the basis for an official report in any form.

b. Cheating: Giving or receiving aid on a test or examination. Test or examination includes any work performed for which a grade is received. Plagiarism is a violation of the Honor Code.

c. Stealing: Taking without authority personal, government or college property.

d. Failing to report a case of lying, cheating, or stealing as defined above to the proper Honor Committee authorities.

(NOTE: For those who are counting, Section III, (4.), states three rules; then subparagraphs 5. a-d enumerate four. This technical incongruence was one more thing that required coping.)

The Honor Code was an initiative by General Clark. It existed in a system owned and operated by the cadets. The system was apparently popularly accepted by the Corps in the '50s and by my time in the '60s, it was a major, time-honored tradition.

For four years, my life hovered at the maw of those two books like a dragon fly flitting around the beak of a mute and motionless snapping turtle.

Violations of *The Blue Book* were often and reoccurring; punishments were awarded frequently and liberally. But proven violations of the Honor Code were very unlikely and would happen only once in a cadet's career. The punishment was the reason that another violation would not occur: an immediately expelled cadet would not have a second chance.

The simplicity of the code – a cadet does not lie, cheat or steal, and does not tolerate such behavior by others – was chiseled starkly wherever I went. I didn't need a book because the words were engraved in my brain.

I knew from the start that the honor system was no nonsense. But as a freshman, it first became real on a Sunday evening in January, 1963 when I returned to the barracks from first semester break. My older brother was with me and somehow in conversation, I realized that I had a target on my back: when I had completed final exams, I had not signed out for the few days of semester break leave as *The Blue Book* required.

39. – REPORTING

39.04. DEPARTURE OF AND RETURN FROM LEAVE AND FURLOUGH: Every cadet who leaves the campus except on general leave will report his departure and return through the guardhouse.

My signature with the signing-out date should have been in the barracks guardroom log days earlier. Now, I had no line for signing that I had returned. If I didn't sign and date that I was present, I would be officially absent without leave. If I were to sign my name and date anything other than the truth in the guard room log, my signature would indict me by the demands of the Honor Code. This was my first truly serious (stupid and unintentional) dilemma with *The Blue Book* and *The Honor Manual*.

My brother first pointed out the serious and stupid parts. To be sure I understood, he emphasized my stupidity several more times. Then he said he would take care of it. My assignment was to not go into the guardroom, ask no questions, and forever remain silent.

I was just a knob. I didn't know what would happen next but I trusted big bubba. I never heard officially from this potentially disastrous mistake. On a day much later, I learned that the page in the log that should have recorded my exiting signature was slit away, as by a pocket knife. The missing page then became someone else's problem to explain. I never found this remedy in my edition of *The Blue Book*, but I am glad it apparently was in my big brother's upper class version.

In my sophomore year, I again found myself flitting between the two blue books. The last royal ruler of Italy, King Umberto II, reigned for a month before the post-war wave of democracy swept *lo Stivale*. Apparently the King and General Clark were wartime buds and the now-presidential General invited the some-time King to come to the college as a distinguished guest. In the incident that resulted, I was more of a counsel for the defense than a perp.

During a rainy noon formation, the first sergeant informed the company that a contingent of "volunteers" would be required to attend an address by the former king of Italy in the chapel. This was followed by the naming of the volunteers. I don't know how these royal subjects were selected. I do remember that most were freshmen and sophomores with a few upper classmen and that the event was to occur in a few hours. Also, I was not among the chosen and the roster was only orally stated, not documented.

One of those who was informed that he had volunteered was my roommate. At the appointed hour, he joined the forlorn representatives from each of the four 3rd Battalion companies forming up in the rain. Formations in the rain were always problematic. Everybody looked the same in their long grey raincoats with hat brims pulled low. No attendance reports were obtained by the cadets in charge and none was submitted to the Commandant from the companies. It seemed that the whole operation was spontaneous.

I watched the contingents from each company begin the march by columns toward the sally port, bemused at my roommate's bad luck and grateful for my providential pardon. Then I witnessed an unforgettable moment.

"ich bin hier".

(The) Shako,
Spring, 1965

As the companies passed into the gloom of the sally port arches, shadowy deserters began to trickle into the void. By the time M Company brought the rear of the column into the passage, the trickle had become a tide. It was dark and wet, but if you were watching like I was, you would have had the impression that a large family of cockroaches in the basement was scurrying into inky obscurity. In another moment, one of those bugs made it back to our room. The problem came the next day.

11. – CHAPEL AND RELIGIOUS SERVICES

11.02. CADETS LEAVING CHAPEL:

b. Cadets leaving Chapel for any reason before the conclusion of chapel exercises will be reported by their company commanders or squad leaders.

Apparently the pest-control problem in my barracks occurred in the other three battalions as well. The King had spoken to a conspicuously sparse crowd of mostly freshmen and the President was highly agitated at the anemic showing. He wanted answers; particularly, he wanted heads.

30. – OFFENSES

30.01. OFFENSES CLASSIFIED: The offenses for which a cadet shall be punished are divided into categories as follows:

   b. Offenses for which dismissal may be the punishment:

      (4) Disobedience to a command of the President or any superior officer.

First sergeants across the battalions became animated as a result of the General's agitation. Within hours, all of us in M Company were confronted by a question demanding an answer: Were you supposed to be at the King's speech yesterday and if so, were you there?

I wasn't snagged on this particular longline fishing hook but my roommate asked me how he should answer the question. It was then that I remembered *The Blue Book* and found a balm in the President's own recommendation:

The Citadel Code "earnestly commended to all cadets": To be generous and helpful to others and to endeavor to restrain them from doing wrong. – Mark W. Clark, President

Determining that I should be helpful and restraining, I thought maybe the President's wrath could be tempered by a direction from the other blue book. I remembered a relevant passage in *The Honor Manual* and took it off the hook for a confirmation. Sure enough, this is what it said:

SECTION III – The Cadet Honor Code

4. *The Honor Code*: The Honor Code is a code of, by, and for The Corps of Cadets. The code states that a cadet does not lie, cheat, or steal. The code is the heart of the Honor System, and its purpose is to maintain honor and integrity within The Corps.

a. Lying: Making a false official statement. The following procedure will be followed in order to prevent the Honor Code from being utilized as an investigative tool:

(1) No commissioned officer of the staff or of the faculty, member of the guard, or any cadet in an official position will ask a question which will incriminate a cadet unless the asker has prima-facie evidence that the cadet has committed a reportable offense.

(2) If a delinquency report is based upon facts brought out by questioning a cadet, the cadet may request his honor representative to obtain a decision from the Honor Committee as to whether the questions were proper and justified.

(3) In case the question is ruled improper by the Honor Committee, The President will be so advised and he will have the delinquency report destroyed or deleted from the records.

With this assurance from holy writ and feeling unusually "generous and helpful" (as commended by the President) I restrained my roommate and told him that he had been asked an "improper question." Then I referred him to Section III of the manual. He followed its advice and honestly admitted that he should be numbered among the escaping bugs of yesterday. That evening, we two talked with our company honor representative.

(The) Shako,
Spring, 1963

I don't know the details of what happened next in the throne room. But at some point, I learned that the crowd which ducked the King's speech also ducked being charged with "an offense for which dismissal may be the punishment." All of them.

SHE SAID IT WAS AN IMPROPER GUESTION.

I first sensed a sort of calling to become an active player in the honor system in my freshman year. But a year later, the King Umberto debacle with its subsequent legal machinations quickened my sense of pre-destination.

In the late spring of my sophomore year, I engaged an aspect of the honor system which was truly oppressive and which I would ultimately score against as a senior. It was a dilemma that occurred when a requirement of *The Blue Book* interfaced with a principle of *The Honor Manual*. The question was for the Commandant: Could he properly rely on the honesty of a cadet who was trying to abide by the Honor Code to produce self-imposed enforcement of cadet regulations as ordered by *The Blue Book*?

If there was ever a helicopter parent of young men, it was the Commandant. He seemed interested in where I was at all times and counted on me to report my presence and absence. He was the chief of the "college authorities" mentioned in the following regulation:

1. – THE CHARACTER OF THE COLLEGE

1.01. SUPERVISION: The Citadel is essentially a Military college, and the college authorities promise parents (or guardians of cadets) that strict control will be complete in so far as is possible.

Part of my participation in his snooping was in complying with certain *Blue Book* regulations. The oppressive monitoring of my location began at my room door in the barracks with a schedule card.

3. - ABSENCE AND CLASS SCHEDULE CARDS

3.01. LOCATION: Each room occupied by one or more cadets will have an absence card, bearing the names of the occupants, in the holder on the door.

3.02. ABSENCE: The absence card will be rigged with a button of appropriate size as an indicator. This indicator will be adjusted to show the duty or general place where the cadet may be found when not in his room. When present in his room, the card will be unmarked.

My name on my card aligned with a horizontal line of possible places I might be other than my room. These places (or circumstances) included the "Library" and "Leave." From my name, a horizontal string was extended along these possible, named destinations. A moveable button was on the string; it indicated where I was in my severely restricted travels. My job was to keep the button on the appropriate mark and to actually be where I indicated I could be found. By the Honor Code, the button's position was an official statement, so it had better be over the target.

I earnestly tried to keep the Commandant updated as to my whereabouts as a freshman. Adjusting the button eventually became a habit as I came and went through my door. My travel around campus was usually rote until the late spring of my sophomore year. That was when I became more involved in extracurricular activities. My first meeting with the Round Table then produced a pang of conscience.

13. CLUBS, SOCIETIES, AND RELATED GROUPS

13.02. GROUP MEETINGS:

b. Cadets going to group meetings under specific authorization during Evening Study Period will sign-out of Barracks through the Guard Room, giving the time of their departure. They will go directly to the group meeting and to no other place. Upon leaving the group meeting they will return directly to Barracks and sign-in through the Guardroom. Cadets will be in their rooms by 2015 hours.

The regimental commander my sophomore year had a reputation such that, if someone had yelled, "Look! Up in the sky – it's a bird – it's a plane…" I would not have been surprised to see that it was the regimental commander. He was an upright, handsome senior cadet on the Round Table when I joined other new members of the group for its last meeting of the year.

I had signed out of Number 3 barracks guardroom a few minutes before 7:00 p.m. (1900 hours) for the meeting in the library. In the last part of the meeting, the Round Table cadets for the next year selected officers for the fall semester. That's when I learned that I was appointed secretary. After the meeting, the regimental commander told me that he had the journal kept by the secretary in his room in Number 2 barracks. I should leave with him to obtain the book.

I had a moment of hesitation as we left the library and approached the parade ground to cross over to his barracks. (Sophomores were among the unwashed who were forbidden to walk such shortcuts.) Then a larger boogeyman spooked me: I was signed out for the library, not Number 2 barracks! 2015 hours was only a few minutes away. If I returned to my barracks to keep my paperwork straight before going to Number 2 barracks, I would eventually be late returning from the meeting – and so on.

Sophomore on the parade ground.

(The) Shako,
Spring, 1964

My distinguished companion was amiable and seemed to not notice my predicament which he had initiated. He was my commander and I was doing as he had directed. I crossed the parade ground with him in silence. I was briefly in his room, then out the sally port, down the walk and into my barracks guardroom to beat the clock. As I signed my name, I wondered if there would be another shoe to drop.

There wasn't. There was however, some tachycardia and perspiration.

In my senior year, I was the honor representative for M Company. As a cadet with a home in Charleston, I had an unusual opportunity to actually influence a change concerning the way the Commandant's Department operated, as it used the honor system to assure compliance with monitoring regulations. The focus of this moment concerned "leave" policy. Mysteriously, the regulation referenced is the only one printed in *The Blue Book of 1960* with words which are highlighted in bold fonts:

27. – LEAVES

27.01. GENERAL INSTRUCTIONS: Leave is a **privilege** (*sic*) extended to the Corps for the purpose of affording individual cadets time away from the institution to accomplish personal business, recreation, job interviews and other activities which require an extended absence from the campus.

It was possible for cadets who qualified academically and had no punishment restrictions to obtain authorization for several weekend leaves ("overnights") each semester. A lot of my friends were from parts unknown and without transportation. For them, Charleston was a desirable destination when they could secure an overnight leave. But *The Blue Book* presented them with a hiccup (as usual.) The Commandant was concerned that a loose twenty-year-old might make a mistake in judgment when out and about locally, overnight without a chaperone. This evil was avoided by restricting cadets on overnights in Charleston to either their own local homes or to Charleston homes with married hostesses:

e. Cadets whose homes **are not** (*sic*) in the greater Charleston area (25 miles radius of campus) and who desire to spend their weekend leaves in Charleston must provide the office of the Commandant in each instance with a written invitation from a married adult host or hostess.

(For the uninitiated, I should clarify that this married adult host or hostess was clearly not the spouse of the cadet requesting leave because of another regulation):

16. – CONDUCT

16.04. GENERAL RULES GOVERNING CONDUCT

s. Married: If any cadet shall be married while in the college, he shall be discharged immediately.

As the son of a naval officer, I had endured a nomadic existence, moving and changing schools about every two to four years. For military records purposes, my "permanent address" had been that of my grandparents' residence in

Charleston my whole life. By this, The Citadel authorities considered me a Charlestonian. When my immediate family moved back to Charleston after my sophomore year and my father left for Vietnam, my grandparents' home remained my official address. This status of mine as a Charlestonian initiated an ethical dilemma when I was the company executive officer.

One of my routine duties as exec was to initial all communications to the Commandant which originated in the company. In this endless paper stream were requests for weekend leaves. It was my initials on certain of these leave requests that caused my heartburn as possible honor violations loomed:

SECTION III – The Cadet Honor Code

5. *Violations of the Code*:

a. Lying: Making a false official statement. An official statement is defined as a statement, written or oral, made to a commissioned officer of the staff or of the faculty of the college, or a guard on duty, or any cadet required, in turn, to use the statement as the basis for an official report in any form.

d. Failing to report a case of lying, cheating, or stealing as defined above to the proper Honor Committee authorities.

In those first few weeks of September, I became troubled by friends whose homes were beyond the pale and so asked if they could sign out to my grandparents' residence. My first response was to tell them that if they did, they had to promise to go by the residence and visit my grandmother and I didn't want to know anything else about their experiences over the weekend. This would ease my conscience as I initialed their leave requests, even though I suspected that their overnights would more likely be spent in a Charleston motel or beach house.

I didn't like this part of my job, either as a cadet officer or as an honor representative. I knew I was probably indirectly facilitating deceit, even if it was not provable - reporting this to the committee for a solution from the Commandant was the answer.

I suspected that the issue of cadets in Charleston on overnights was not limited to M Company. Sure enough, when I presented the problem to my classmates on the Honor Committee, they all said it was a problem across the Corps. So we composed a letter to the Commandant which represented the widespread practice of fudging on Charleston overnight leave requests. In the message, we emphasized the stress of the dilemma for conscientious cadets trying to do their jobs.

Preserved in The Citadel Archives is a letter that shined brightly in 1965, even as it remained unknown in the Corps. I first read it many years later.

The letter was written to the Commandant from the President (Gen. H.P. Harris, at the time.) It reads, in part:

"In my view, the honor code is separate and distinct from the ordinary disciplinary requirements. The [honor] *system cannot survive in accomplishing its purposes if overburdened by routine matters or overzealous effort to attain strict discipline from a military viewpoint. The system is a part of the moral tone we wish to foster – not only on the campus but in the individual after the cadet leaves this environment. For this reason I do not wish to have certificates required or to have implied violations of honor based on such things as leaving their rooms and where they may go. The simple application of this system is that the cadet must not consciously lie, cheat or steal. There are many actions which can be violations of our regulations but the only direct connection with the honor code is when such violation has been discovered, or thought to be discovered, and the individual is confronted with the allegation. I expect that you will administer an effective disciplinary system without dependence on the honor code."*

As a result of our persuasion, *The Blue Book* regulation (27.01. - e) was cancelled that fall by an official announcement and order. The order changed nothing about the fact that cadets were staying in Charleston for general leave, regardless of their hometowns. But you would have had to be a cadet just walking across campus or signing official papers to know the relief this brought as the searchlights of the Honor Code swept somewhere else around the compound.

Honor Court proceedings my senior year were not frequent – but they were always serious and sometimes tragic in outcome. They often continued into the late night but finished before *Reveille*. Accused cadets were usually represented legally by their company representatives. I don't remember actual attorneys being in the court sessions. The President reviewed the record of the proceedings the next morning and if the cadet were to be convicted, he would be gone before the end of the day. Sometimes I would hear second-hand that "there was an honor hearing last night," but usually I heard nothing at all.

All-nighters in the courtroom, along with other responsibilities, occasionally left me with a sleep deficit which demanded a remedy. I found the solutions through my cordial business relationship with Colonel Courvoisie. I write this first-of-all, to relate an emotionally trying moment for me as a senior and secondly, to finish my tale of woe concerning a bug on my hat as it pertained to the Honor Code.

In the second semester, one of my roommates told me that he was slipping off campus for a few hours after the *Call to Quarters* division check. In the parlance, this was called "breaking barracks," a "first class" offense:

30. – OFFENSES

30.01. OFFENSES CLASSIFIED:

c. Offenses of the First Class:

(6) Going beyond cadet limits without leave.

I said to him, "You know I will have to report you absent if a tac comes through." He knew that, he said. He also reassured he wouldn't hold it against me. So he broke barracks that evening and a tac came by, and I told the truth.

The next day, I was so distraught over reporting my roomie absent that I had to tell someone. So I asked permission to speak with Colonel Courvoisie. I told the Colonel the circumstance of the last evening, then I said, "I wanted you to know that I reported my roommate because of the Honor Code, not out of duty."

I'll never forget the momentary frown, the pause, and then his softly spoken response: "I'm really disappointed in you, Bubba."

I asked," Will that be all, sir?" It was. I saluted and left.

The Boo was a Citadel graduate, a WW2 vet, and a member of the Greatest Generation. He was the Assistant Commandant overseeing the practical aspects of cadet discipline. I respected him and enjoyed his sense of humor. He seemed to know of my literary expressions in cadet publications and I thought that he respected me. So then there was the bug story I related earlier. I left it hanging, with him confiscating the evidence and awarding me demerits as I remained silent and accepting.

21. – EXPLANATIONS

21.01. WHEN MADE:

a. Every report made against a cadet will be recorded on a delinquency list posted on the company bulletin board.

b. Any report may be explained by the cadet against whom it is made. Whenever a report is incorrect or needs clarification in the interest of justice, it should be explained. A written explanation of all reports having an "H" in the award column is required.

A few days after I was debugged by the Boo, I read on the company delinquency list that I had been awarded five demerits for "Bug on hat." I don't remember thinking about this at the time, but it could have turned much darker because of the demands of the honor system.

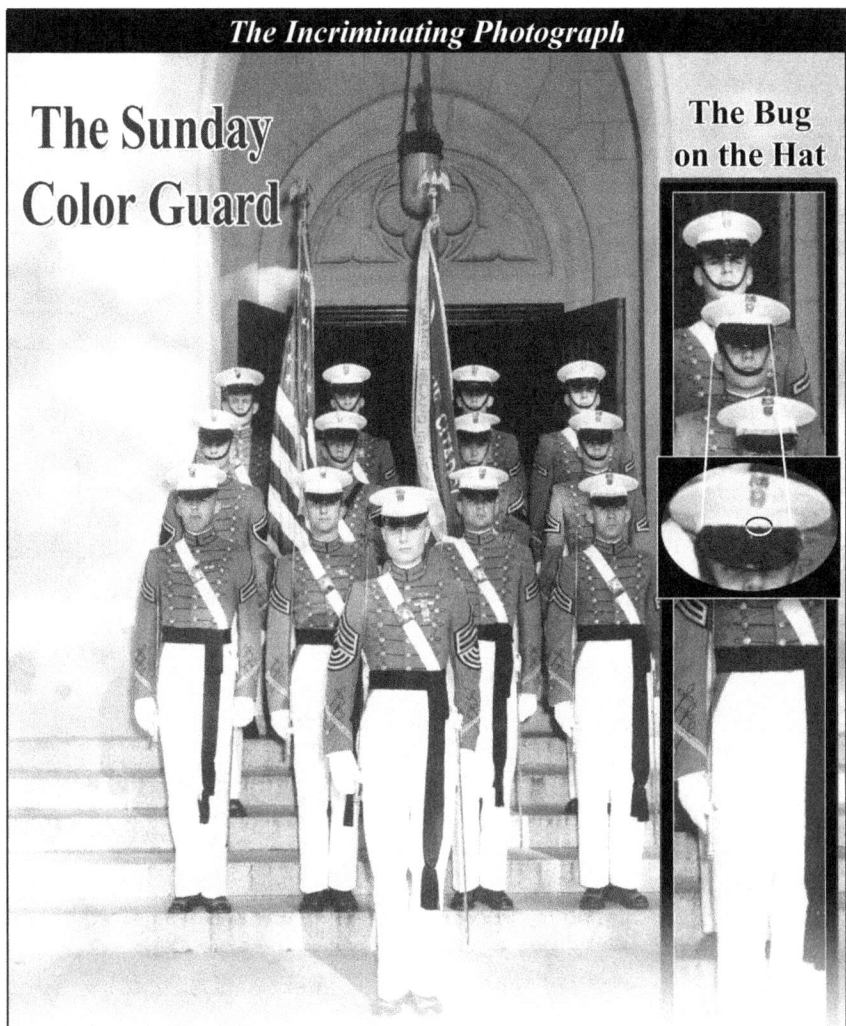

The Incriminating Photograph

The Sunday Color Guard

The Bug on the Hat

*Like the other photographs offered in this book, this one is an original print in my (very modest) private collection. I do not remember how or when I acquired this image that was published in **The Sphinx of 1965**. The classmate who took many of the images in the 1966 yearbook and developed them himself, is standing near me in the photograph. So he may have been an accomplice. The image contains the forensic proof that I was actually wearing the bug in the spring of 1965. It is centered at the top margin of the black leather strap on my hat. The Boo nailed me a year later.*

Ordinarily, this particular offense would probably not have resulted simply in the award of demerits. The delinquency list was far more likely to read "H" beside the charge because "Bug on hat" was such an unusual report. Bugs got on hats occasionally and the solution was to flick them off. What would cause a Colonel to charge a cadet with "Bug on hat?" The Commandant's curiosity would likely require an explanation in writing from me – an infamous ERW.

My sensitivity over this thought is probably a minor PTSD reaction. The symptoms trouble me when I remember those days as M Company executive officer, reading and initialing endless ERWs.

21. – EXPLANATIONS

21.02. HOW SUBMITTED:

When a written explanation is made it will be submitted with the appropriate delinquency list to the Commandant of Cadets by the Cadet First Sergeant. Company Executive Officers will review all explanations for clarity, brevity, pertinence and correctness.

I knew the form of the ERW well. I could write one today without a pattern to follow and it would be pretty close to standards.

21.03. CONTENTS OF EXPLANATION:

a. An explanation will consist of a straightforward, clear, and complete recital of facts. It will not contain criticism, complaint, argument, or opinion, or any irrelevant remark or quibbling or denial of a report when a matter of opinion is involved.

d. Every written explanation will state

(1) Whether the report is correct or incorrect.

(2) A brief recital of pertinent facts.

(3) Whether or not the offense was intentional or that there was no offense.

The two requirements – that the ERW must include a direct agreement or disagreement with the report itself, and that the truth of intentionality be faced by the accused – were critical to the stark inspection of the document. In theology and jurisprudence, the agreement that the report is correct is called "confession" which both the Bible and the Boo would endorse as good for the soul.

The idea of whether or not the offense was intentional is a confrontation with the source of the underlying motivation. In the Bible, unintentional sins in the Hebrew religious system could be remedied through temple sacrifices. But there was not a remedy for intentional sin. Except for the mercy of God, the Hebrew guilty of intentional sin was to be "cut off" (typically, stoned to death; see Numbers 15:30.)

There is a Hebrew word that distinguishes intentional sin from other violations of the law in the *Tanakh* (that is, the Hebrew Bible.) In various English translations of Psalm 19:13, this word may be expressed as "deliberate," "willful," or "presumptuous." In context, these words describe an inner attitude of defiance which motivates a misbehavior. I detour into these points of biblical wisdom as a preparation for reconsidering the case of, "Bug on hat," according to the book that regulates my life today.

When the Boo spotted the bug, I handed him my hat. As he extracted the stick pin, he shot me through with his famous squint, drew near with his cigar breath, and seethed, "Your heart is black, bubba."

There was no rule against having a bug on your hat. It wasn't really a bug anyway. Yet, I knew I was properly in a moment of judgment and had no recourse but to trust in the mercy of the judge.

21.05. ARGUMENTS AND DISCUSSIONS:

Written explanations are submitted in the interest of justice. A cadet will not argue with a reporting officer or attempt to discuss any report with him except by his express permission.

21.06. QUIBBLING:

Quibbling is prohibited. Attempting to avoid punishment by evading the issue by virtue of the report being inaccurate as to date, time, or spelling of name, and similar reasons, is a punishable offense.

I had nothing, so I said nothing. He kept the bug and gave me back my hat. I saluted as he dismissed me and the moment passed. But would there now be an ERW? Was the report of "Bug on hat" correct or incorrect? Was the offense intentional – or unintentional – or was there no offense?

In my black heart, I knew that the report was correct and that the offense was intentional. To confess to deliberately and presumptuously wearing a lady bug pin on my hat was to admit a mockery of the authorities who continuously inspected me and was the No. 1, First Class offense listed in *The Blue Book*:

30. – OFFENSES

30.01. OFFENSES CLASSIFIED:

c. Offenses of the First Class:

(1) Insubordination; disrespectful, refractory, or disorderly conduct.

If I had an "H" on the delinquency list beside the report of "Bug on hat," my ERW would have been at a minimum, honest. An honest confession of insubordination that late in my senior year could have produced a disastrous award in an official report.

But on the company delinquency list a few days later there was only an award of five demerits beside "Bug on hat." The Boo had spared me the misery of an explanation. I'm sure this mercy was because he saw where it would go. With no ERW required, there would be no need to confront my presumptuous sin in writing. He probably enjoyed leaving the rest to my conscience.

Oh – and the Boo was right. My well-trained heart had done the best it could to obey. But it was black. This I realized more as years passed and I remembered my Creator beyond the days of my youth. I was learning the truth about the whole man from the book that has guided my life since those days:

> **This is the judgment that the Light has come into the world, and men loved the darkness rather than the Light, for their deeds were evil.** - John 3:19 (NASB, 2020)

The spring of 1966 was a serious season for Citadel seniors. We were hearing every now and then of the combat deaths of people we knew in the recently graduated classes. I knew no one who spoke of avoiding military service. But we were often considering ourselves and our friends and what the underclasses would be hearing about us this time next year. I was having somber thoughts like these when I put the final draft of *The 1966 Sphinx* to bed with this dedication:

> *"A college can do no more than educate and train. It is her sons who must ultimately prove the validity of this preparation. In the peace and war of over a century, The Citadel man has been required to expand this groundwork laid for him by his school and has pointed with particular pride to the battle streamers which demanded that Citadel blood be given.*
>
> *Today the place is Vietnam. The land is as complicated as are the reasons for the United States fighting for it. But one over-riding factor is sufficient for Citadel men to fight and die once again: this is where we make our stand. To The Citadel men in Vietnam, the 1966 Sphinx is dedicated."*

My year of graduation – 1966 - was at the end of an era in American history and the beginning of another. The war was looking very serious, even though it was still officially only a "conflict." Students in distant colleges were in the streets and young men my age were dodging to Canada to avoid the draft.

Over the next few years, I was a medical student living with my wife who used to be my girl. These were the years of the Summer of Love, the Age of Aquarius, and the Civil Rights era. Flower children drove around in decorated VW vans with bumper stickers reading, "Question Authority," directly challenging the contemporary leadership of the Greatest Generation.

During this time, as I was learning pharmacology and physical diagnosis, my roomie, Tom, was in serious military combat training. In our last two years of college, I came to know Tom as a big, strong cat, restless and caged in the pen called the 3rd Battalion barracks. We never discussed the future, but we both knew that we would likely be commissioned army officers and that our futures would begin when we returned from the war.

Details of my years of medical training and residency are hard to remember. I did serve in the Army eventually as a Captain, but by then the war was winding down and young medical officers were no longer needed in the war zone. The troops returning were largely wrecked emotionally and they were coming home to families that were drifting away in a chaotic society. Young doctors with no more experience than I had were more valuable to the Army at home, trying to heal this social carnage. So for two years, I defended the eastern front in a little clinic on Virginia Beach where all was quiet.

But Tom went to Tan Son Nhut Air Base where he learned he was to become a platoon leader in the 1st Air Cav. I heard from him sometimes and would write back when I did - I still treasure his letters. His letters were light and hopeful and, if not for the dreary nightly news on TV (which too often featured the 1st Air Cavalry Division), it would have been easy to believe that he was watching the war from a safe distance. Tom eventually came home, married and became a general contractor, then a longshoreman.

For forty years and more, we lived near each other and remained good friends. But Tom got in trouble in his marriage and developed some serious health problems. Eventually he lived alone and the government determined that he was totally disabled. Tom became a frequenter of VA clinics and I was in pain as I saw his health fading. Along the way, he confided once that he was diagnosed with PTSD related to his combat experiences and he was in a group for therapy.

I processed the information as a doctor would, and nodded. Group therapy was standard for treating PTSD. We continued our unspoken policy of not discussing the war or his condition.

My friend had more bad days than good as the years passed and he was on too many important medications. He had become forgetful and distracted and – feeble. When he had no medical appointments, Tom bunkered in his apartment beside his black Labrador retriever, digesting television news. He called me when too much time had passed (me, the busy doctor), invariably apologizing for his loneliness and wondering what I was "up to." Such calls usually resulted in lunch or a drive in the countryside. One moment was unforgettable and worth recalling:

We were the same age, yet he was much older when I took him out for coffee that day. The warm cup felt good in my hands as we huddled on the patio of the shop and discussed the news. Tom mentioned that the former president who was almost ninety years old had parachuted out of an airplane the day before, just because he could. For President Bush, it was a moment to relive his adventure in the Second World War when his plane was splashed over the Pacific.

I don't know why, but I asked, "Were you airborne qualified in Vietnam?"

"No," said Tom. Then he added thoughtfully, "But I was assigned to lead a special mission once that was an airborne operation. We were about to take off when the top sergeant asked me if I had ever jumped before. I told him that I hadn't and wondered why he asked."

"He said, 'Lieutenant, you're wearing your parachute wrong and it won't work like that.' Tom chuckled and continued, "I was pulled from the assignment."

Without thinking, I violated our policy: "You were in the 1st Air Cav and not qualified to jump. Your commander must have known that."

Tom replied, "I was an infantry platoon leader. I loved being out in the woods alone and I had an ability to figure out where I was on the ground, even in the dark. So I was on the roster of a 'rapid response' team. When they needed a small group to get some specific job done quickly, I might get called for that."

"So you didn't go that time."

"No - but I went often enough. I remember once we had a call from a forward recon team that an NVA headquarters had been located near the Cambodian border. I was one of ten or twelve guys who went in response."

"So....I guess by helicopter?"

"Yeah."

"At night?"

"Yeah. We came down in a rice paddy and the pilot pointed me toward a tree line. I remember how quiet it was after the chopper pulled away and how bright the stars seemed. We set up a perimeter in the brush. I told my top sergeant that I would go alone to find the location of the headquarters; we'd figure out a plan when I returned."

"I went on into the woods for a while, pretty sure of the direction. Eventually I saw a light which came from a campfire. There were several NVA officers at the fire with some women. They looked like they were drinking and partying in front of a hooch. I didn't see any guards. I decided I could get the job done and get back to my squad, so I did."

"You…"

"I shot all of them."

"I guess you got back okay."

"Yeah."

"So, what did you tell your men?"

"They were all dead."

"And what did they say?"

"Who?"

"Your men."

"They were all dead."

I swallowed and became a professional. "Oh. So, what did you do?"

"I lay down beside them and waited for sunrise. I knew the recon team was nearby and that the chopper would be back."

"I guess you got out okay."

"Yeah. I left the area with the recon team."

I thought before I spoke: "Was this the event that is associated with your PTSD?"

"No. That was something else."

We both knew that the policy was now to be followed again. Our group meeting was canceled for now – too many members were missing. We finished our coffee and I drove my old friend home. He never spoke of the incident again.

Five years later, I was there with a group of M Company classmates when he was re-baptized in his apartment's bathroom sink. I read in his obituary that he had been awarded the Silver Star. Tom had never mentioned the award to me.

Tom was a leader when he was a freshman among the rest of us. His talent and character shone brightly during our few years together and I now realize that his strength was in his humility. With the self-control of a member of the Junior Sword Drill, he was ready to serve. With his humility, he was willing and available to be a Cadet Captain when he could have been a Colonel. Even with all of Tom's troubles, I believe General Clark would have seen his "whole man" if he had looked up in the sky at Tom.

I practiced general pediatrics in North Charleston for almost forty years. During this time, I served on the medical staff of several hospitals and was the doctor for the children of a number of hospital staff professionals. Among these was a hospital administrator who had been a freshman in M Company when I was a junior. He and I had become reacquainted when Pat Conroy's novel about The Citadel, *The Lords of Discipline*, became controversial in Charleston.

My administrator friend asked me if I had read Conroy's new book. I had not. I told him that I knew Pat Conroy as a cadet, I had read several of his books, and appreciated his gift as a wordsmith. I just didn't care to read his latest because those days were still too close. He said I should read it and then offered his copy which he had just finished.

So I read it – that is, I tried to read it. I often could read no more than a few pages without having to lay it down and walk away for a while. It wasn't because of the story – that was fiction. It was that the sights, the sounds, and the smells were too real.

When I finished the book, I returned it to this friend and fellow professional who was a father in my medical practice. I included a hand-written note of apology along with the book. I barely remembered him as a knob and had no memory of any unpleasantness between him and me. But I told him that if I had ever done anything that was personally offensive to him, I truly regretted it and asked for forgiveness. His reaction was to give a little sympathetic chuckle. He reassured me that there was nothing to forgive and we carried on as before.

After I completed medical training, I became a teacher of the Bible. It is the wisdom of this book that now directs my own journey to becoming a whole man. By *The Blue Book of 1960*, I confronted fear and anger as I practiced self-control. Over years of further medical training, I then began to lose even awareness of just experiencing emotions. Too many hard experiences in neonatal and pediatric ICUs had demonstrated the liability of my emotions in doing my work well.

By biblical rehab, I eventually realized that I had made a mistake when I included compassion on my list of lost emotions. I admitted the necessity to call on God to restore compassion in my life and I remember when He did it. I was in a moment of suturing a little laceration on the eyebrow of a toddler who disagreed with the medical care he was receiving. I was making my move and he was struggling against my stronger and more determined office nurse when suddenly, I couldn't see the cut or the suture needle. That's when I realized that my eyes were filled with tears. Tears! God had given me compassion again.

Beyond office and hospital pediatrics, I practiced medicine among aboriginal people in the Amazon forest of eastern Ecuador on several occasions. Then the attacks of 9-11 compelled me to train for disaster relief: I just had to be part of whatever happened next. When I qualified, I joined a medical group on-call.

On the day we learned of the earthquake at Port-au-Prince, I told my wife that I would likely go with a disaster relief team to Haiti. News reports over the next days were alarming. Tens of thousands of people had died and hundreds of thousands were stranded with nothing, including medical care.

When my team was called, there were no direct flights to Port-au-Prince. We spent a day on a dusty bus, bouncing along from Santo Domingo to the earthquake zone. I was already winded when we arrived that evening at a missionary station in a residential area. It was the only building still standing in a crowded neighborhood of pancaked houses, crushed cars, sparking utility lines, and collapsed stone walls.

The front porch of our barracks was unstable. Inside, it was crowded with volunteers like me – engineers, well-drillers, electricians and road builders from all across the U.S. My room was too small and cramped with too many double bunks. Creole meals were served by Haitians and bathroom facilities were minimal. The daily medical work was difficult and I was glad to loosen my boots each evening.

I had been a doctor in Haiti before – it was badly broken then and the earthquake had not improved the place. Everything was cement dust gray. My medical facility was in a little church with no roof beside a teeming refugee camp. My interpreter told me his home was a pile of rocks, draped with a blue U.N. tarp. His sister was in Miami, having her legs amputated.

I quickly fell into a routine in this crowded society of strangers. I kept my gear orderly and under the bunk, ate trail mix instead of the thick, spicy food, and shaved early, before the others stirred. In the dark of one morning, I found the little bathroom empty and slipped inside. I noticed an odor, then realized that the floor, the tub and the toilet were generously spackled with the contents of some volunteer's stomach. Too much *manje Ayisien* for supper, I supposed.

115

I was experienced in third world situations. Dealing with a medical mess was part of the work and necessary to keep the standard. So I walked over to the relief coordinators who were intently working on their computers near a window. The glow from their laptop screens was the only light.

"The bathroom's a mess," I said from the dark. "Please tell me where I can find a mop and some Clorox."

"We know about it. The girl will take care of it."

That was it? The girl? The Haitians were suffering enough without having to clean up some American's mess. I felt anger I had not experienced in years rise up. My overseers were unaware of my reaction. I had nothing else to say and it was very dark.

I turned to search for the cleaning materials and found a closet with the necessary stuff. With a mop and a sponge, I cleaned up the remnants of stewed tomato, onion, peppers, garlic and beans, then sprinkled a little extra Clorox around.

After the bathroom was in order, I took some time to nurse my anger. I was mad at the guy who didn't clean up his own mess; I was mad at the leaders. But mostly, I was mad at American arrogance. With daylight, I was packing medicines when an elderly Alabama volunteer approached and asked if I might be a doctor. Her husband was upstairs sick and she asked if I would help.

My patient was the perp. He tried to be welcoming as he told me he became sick last night after supper. His experience in the bathroom was so violent that he could only crawl back to his room. Now he was too weak to get out of his bunk. Cramps and vomiting last night. Better now. He hated to bother me.

I listened, asked some questions…examined him. "You are dehydrated," I said to him. "But I think the worst has passed. If you can sip fluids and hold them down during the day, you'll be okay." We made some arrangements and contingency plans. He thanked me and asked if he could say a brief prayer for me, before I left for the day.

In that moment, prayer was the last thing on my list. But I said "Thank you" and he prayed a wonderful prayer, focused on the Lord helping me. On my way out, I found some oral rehydration fluids, spoke with his wife, and joined my team in the truck. That was when words from the book that had guided me long before *The Blue Book* coagulated somewhere inside:

> **"Then the Lord said to Cain, 'Why are you angry? And why is your face gloomy? If you do well, will your face not be cheerful? And if you do not do well, sin is lurking at the door; and its desire is for you, but you must master it.'"** – Genesis 4:6 (NASB, 2020)

As we bounced across the ruins of Port-au-Prince in the dark of the canvas-covered army truck, I felt the warmth of shame creeping across the back of my neck. Then I wiped away a tear. I was wrong to blame him; I was wrong to blame them. It was *my* pride that troubled me – not theirs. The Boo had been right about my heart.

There was no ERW required, but in silence, I confessed that the report was correct and asked for help. This next part is as real as *The Blue Book* on my shelf: The anger was gone and in an instant, I was okay.

My class of 1966 had its fiftieth reunion some years ago. I still try to meet monthly with Charleston area classmates for lunch. Almost every meeting, someone I haven't seen since graduation drops by. Most of us were military officers and many are combat veterans. We talk about grandkids and whatever happened to whoever. Our meetings always open with a grace being spoken by some itinerant preacher among us. I am gratified that so many of us think this part matters.

On one occasion, three guys from the 1st Battalion spoke authoritatively and were in agreement about the Commandant's "infinitesimal one percent" speech. They said that his speech in the mess hall that day was actually the second time they had heard it. The first time was during a practice parade when the Commandant called to their cadet commander to bring his massed company to a halt. He then strode directly to the last rank and addressed the senior privates. That was when they learned that *they* were the infinitesimal 1%. The rest of us first learned of our minority status in the mess hall the next day. For all of us, it was still a point of satisfaction.

So I told them that after graduation, I had a visit with the Boo. On that quiet afternoon at his home, he thoughtfully commented, "You know bubba, when you were a cadet, we had our eye on you. We knew you were up to something."

"Me? Colonel, I wasn't up to anything. I was just trying to stay alive in my little hole in the wall."

"No - you were up to something. We were a lot more worried about you than we were Conroy."

I really enjoy recalling that moment. *They thought I was up to something. Hmmm.*

117

A Thought beyond *The Blue Book*

From *The Blue Book of 1960*:

DISCIPLINE

To be disciplined does not mean either that one executes orders received only in such measure as seems proper or possible, but it means that one enters freely into the thought and aims of the chief who has ordered, and that one takes every possible means to satisfy him. The first condition to obeying is, therefore, to visualize all the order received and nothing else, then to find the means of complying with it, irrespective of personal opinions, difficulties or obstacles.

MARSHAL FOCH

From *The Bible*, Hebrews 12:5-11 (NASB, 2020):

DISCIPLINE

My son, do not regard lightly the discipline of the Lord, nor faint when you are punished by Him; for whom the Lord loves, He disciplines, and He punishes every son whom he accepts. It is for discipline that you endure; God deals with you as with sons, for what son is there whom his father does not discipline? But if you are without discipline, of which all have become partakers, then you are illegitimate children and not sons. Furthermore, we had earthly fathers to discipline us, and we respected them; shall we not much more be subject to the Father of spirits, and live? For they disciplined us for a short time as seemed best to them, but He disciplines us for our good, so that we may share His holiness. For the moment, all discipline seems not to be pleasant, but painful; yet to those who have been trained by it, afterward it yields the peaceful fruit of righteousness.

YOUR CREATOR

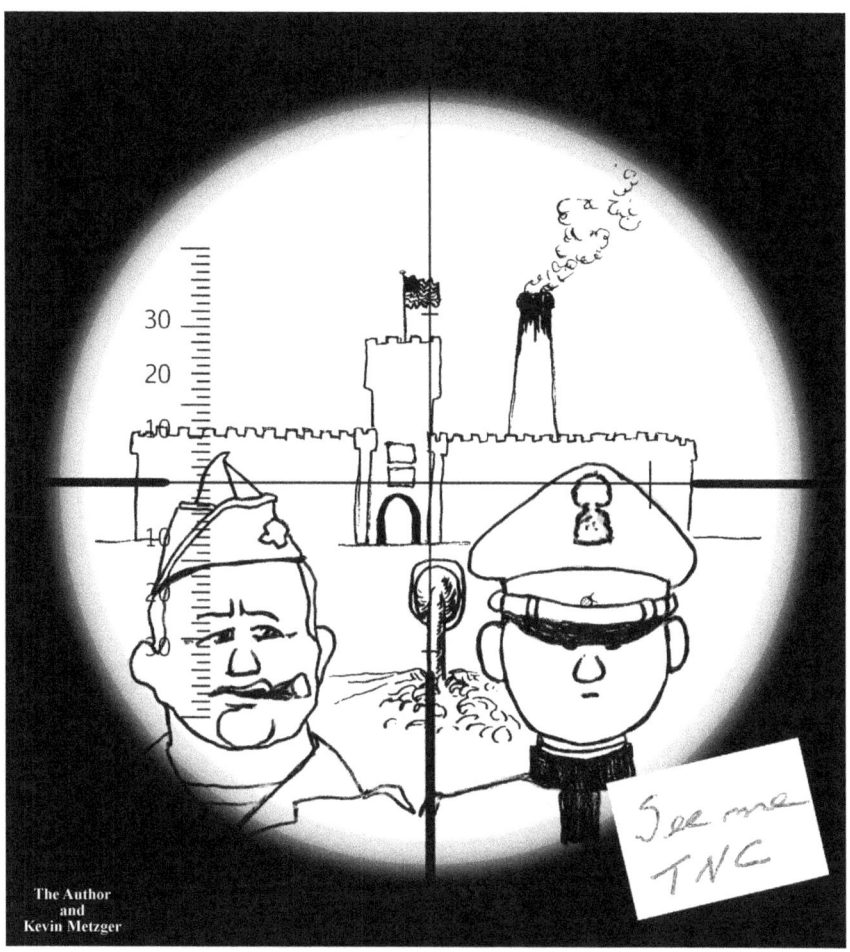

Your heart is black, bubba.

Two More Books and the Whole Man

Bibliography

Books of reference:

Mauldin, Bill; *Up Front;* The World Publishing Company, Cleveland, OH; 1945.

Nicholson, Dennis D.; *A History of The Citadel: The Years of Summerall and Clark*; Published by The Association of Citadel Men, Charleston, SC, 1994.

Quotations from *The Blue Book of 1960* and *The Honor Manual of 1960* are indicated by the distinctive respective formats of these publications. *The Honor Manual of 1960, The Sphinx* (1964 & 1966) and *The Shako* are quoted as published. All of these publications are in the author's collection.

The letter of General Harris, quoted on page 105, is from The Citadel archives, with thanks to classmate Gary Baker.

Except for one cartoon by Bill Mauldin (page 48), the artwork is the author's with occasional assistance from Kevin Metzger. The previously published cartoons were reproduced from materials in the author's collection.

www.ingramcontent.com/pod-product-compliance
Lightning Source LLC
Chambersburg PA
CBHW061655120626
46550CB00003B/948